**THE MORE Y
THE MORE**

THE MORE YOU GIVE, THE MORE YOU GET

Mike Dickson

*To John
With best wishes
Mike*

· THE GENEROUS PRESS ·

First published in Great Britain in 2005 by
The Generous Press, 59A Portobello Road, London W11 3DB

This edition published 2007

© Michael Dickson, 2005, 2007
mikedickson@themoreyougive.co.uk
www.themoreyougive.co.uk

All rights reserved. No part of this publication may be reproduced, stored in a retrieval system, or transmitted in any form or by any means, electronic, mechanical, photocopying, recording, or otherwise without the prior permission in writing of The Generous Press, nor be otherwise circulated in any form of binding or cover other than in which it is published and without a similar condition including this condition being imposed on a subsequent purchaser. The moral right of the author has been asserted.

ISBN: 978-0-9551591-1-4

Contents

Preface 9

Introduction
SERENDIPITY 15

Chapter 1
WHY GIVING IS GOOD FOR YOU 21

Chapter 2
CHARITY BEGINS AT HOME 44

Chapter 3
HOW TO GIVE TO CHARITY 68

Chapter 4
CHARITY WORLD 97

Chapter 5
PHILANTHROPY 142

Chapter 6
CORPORATE GIVING 194

Epilogue 236

Acknowledgements

Many people inspired me while writing this book. The children and many people I met through Whizz-Kidz; the wonderful individuals who give in quiet and often creative ways; several enlightened business leaders; the wisdom expressed in the writings of Tolstoy, George Bernard Shaw, Gandhi, and the teachings of all faiths and beliefs.

The book would never have been possible without the help, support and contributions of many people. To say nothing of their unbelievable patience! To you all, a huge thank you:

Marcia Balisciano; Diana Barran; Nick Barton; Fiona Brown; Howard Carter; Jon Cracknell; Sir Crispin Davis; Harry Duff; Mike de Giorgio; Helen Ewing; Stanley Fink; Fiona Fleming Brown; Patrick Foster; Miko Giedroyc; David Gold; Ben Goldsmith; Virginia Graham; Sarah Greer; Charles and Elizabeth Handy; Rev Mark Hargreaves; Nigel Harris; Lucy Heller; Alexander Hoare; Jeremy Hocking; Sheila Hooper; Sarah Kuehne; Tony Juniper; Sir Peter Lampl; Rachel Leyshon; Susan Mackenzie; Tristan Millington-Drake; Dr Fred Mulder; Michael Norton; Cathy Pharoah; David Pitchford; Russell Prior; Stuart Rose; Jean and Graham Ross Russell; Richard Reed; Benny Refson; Julian Richer; David Robinson; Nat Sloane; Nikki Studt; Michael Spencer; Stefan Velvick. And Google.

*To Shuna, Annabel and William,
who have given me so much*

The more you give,
the more you get
the more you laugh,
the less you fret,
the more you do unselfishly,
the more you live abundantly,
the more of everything you share,
the more you'll always have to spare,
the more you love,
the more you find,
that life is good,
and friends are kind,
for only what we give away,
enriches us from day to day.

— HELEN STEINER RICE

Preface

> 'I believe we have a fundamental human need to give. We all need help in our own lives, we all need to give. At a funeral or memorial service you never hear people say, "He made a lot of money, had three boats." You hear, "He was generous, sincere, always had time for people." Those are the things that we value in others and we value them in ourselves. We feel better for giving.'
>
> David Robinson, founder of Community Links
> and We Are What We Do

It is true, isn't it? We do feel much better about ourselves when we are able to give generously and to help others. We learn more about life – certainly life outside our own very small world. And we don't really *need* all the stuff we buy, accumulate and 'save for a rainy day' anyway, do we?

I would love to think that you will read every brilliant word of this book – but experience shows that you are more likely to read the parts that appeal to you first, then perhaps another chapter, and a few of the stories and profiles.

So here is a little flight plan to help you.

Chapter 1: Why Giving is Good For You

There is a wealth of literature about the importance of having a purpose in life, and all of it recognises that a life without purpose is a life wasted. All the main faiths share this belief, and – contrary to popular opinion – the overwhelming majority of people in this world do have a faith. From Greek philosophers to contemporary management gurus, all are agreed that a purposeful life excludes the need for lashings of money, and finds its true meaning in service to others. So the questions you need to ask yourself are: What is the point of you? What is enough? How do you make the transformation from 'success to significance'? There are a huge number of things that you can choose to do to help others, in this country and around the world. Once you have decided to become useful.

Chapter 2: Charity Begins at Home

I believe giving should start with acts of generosity and kindness to the people you know: your family, friends, colleagues at work. 'Inreach' instead of 'outreach'. Very simple things mean a great deal to most people, often more than the grander acts of giving. In this chapter I explain why we should be thoughtful and gentle to others, and suggest lots of small things you can do to help people. And I also include a few words about forgiveness – forgiving is also giving – and some thoughts about helping people you don't know, or wouldn't usually give the time of day to. To bring out the Good Samaritan in you.

One of the major lessons I re-learned through researching this book is that great and good acts are only achieved by people who are committed to action, not to words or thoughts or views. Save us all from people with views! As Peter Melchett, a past Director of Greenpeace, has said: 'I prefer the optimism of action to the pessimism of thought.' We are what we do, and we can start today by doing lots of little things to help one another. It is soppy, perhaps, but important.

Chapter 3: How to Give to Charity

Giving is a very personal issue. What you actually care about, outside of your normal daily and material concerns, defines you as a human being. What touches your heart or makes you angry? The fact that people are still homeless in the twenty-first century? That young children are abused? That one person dies every three seconds in Africa? That while millions starve in one area of the world, many others are obese and spend small fortunes on diets, fitness regimes and gyms? There is enough in the world to share; it just doesn't get shared.

The secret of effective and enjoyable giving is to focus on the causes that interest you and then to get organised and involved. In this chapter I show you how to do this, as well as review your own giving and make it both more effective and more fun. There are also some thoughts on volunteering, as well as how to organise regular giving that takes advantage of those all-important tax breaks.

Chapter 4: Charity World

Charities are part of the fabric of our society. Having worked in the charity sector for a number of years, I am still surprised by the number of public misconceptions about them. A great many people still believe that every penny of every pound that they give to charity should go directly to the cause, which is insane. How do they expect these important organisations to be managed? I try here to explain a little about the charity world from a layman's point of view and include a few idiosyncratic thoughts on how to start an organisation. I have a slight advantage here in that I actually did start a charity, Whizz-Kidz, which is now successful and useful, so I have practical knowledge of the highs and lows of managing one, of the problems of raising funds and the challenges of distributing them well.

You will also read about the less popular causes – ones that find it hard to get support from the general public, such as charities that deal with addictions of various sorts, domestic violence, difficult and disadvantaged young people, and the environment. You might think you have heard enough about the environment – but for me it was one of the major shocks of my research. It is a hugely complex issue, involving climate change, the forecast growth in the population, the lack of food and water, 'not enough' oil, desertification and more. Contrary to what you might read in the newspapers there is no scientific argument about whether climate change is true or false. It is true, it is happening now, and your life, to say nothing of the lives of your children, is going to change very, very soon.

Chapter 5: Philanthropy

And what about all these new philanthropists who are making headlines? Well, the bottom line is that there *are* a few enlightened people who are giving more, but it is not yet an established trend. Charity income has not increased in real terms in the last ten years, but many people have become seriously wealthy in the same period. Over £26 billion was earned in bonuses in 2006 alone, of which £14 billion was paid out in the financial services sector. There is a real and urgent need to encourage more than the handful who already give to become engaged with the social issues that challenge us, be it the environment, the education of our young people, world poverty or medical research. The enlightened few are actually a) stars b) surprisingly engaged and c) an example to the rest of us, to say nothing of their wealthy friends.

My argument is: if you live in a country that gives you the freedom to create significant wealth for yourself, your family or your business, then you should informally and quietly thank it by helping out some of the poorer sections of society, the community and the world. In my opinion, it is part of the deal.

Anyway, why *wouldn't* you want to do so?

In this chapter there are interviews with UK philanthropists such as Stanley Fink and Sir Peter Lampl, together with some ideas on how to become a philanthropist yourself. Many philanthropists are passionate and professional. They research causes in detail, take an active interest in them and want their donations to make a real impact. Some even start their own foundations.

Chapter 6: Corporate Giving

Not Corporate Social Responsibility, some of which is useful and much of which is nonsense, a 'PR fig leaf'. No, what I am taking about is giving. Money and time and talent.

Could companies give more to society? Should they? The answers are yes and yes, and there is a very good business case for doing so. Companies give very little to charities, an average of 0.2 per cent of their pre-tax profits. Very few business leaders or managers, directors, CEOs and chairmen understand the real business benefits of active involvement with charities. Even those who do give thoughtfully and effectively are hopeless at celebrating or publicising their excellent initiatives. Very often their staff don't even know what good work they do, never mind their customers. The power of a business to do good by motivating its staff and adopting a charity is simply enormous and, for the most part, unrealised. If a company of any size sets out to help a cause, the results can be outstanding. In addition, such work will make it a more intelligent and stronger company, a better place to work, and, in business-speak, 'enhance its shareholder value'. There are some great examples, from Marks & Spencer to Innocent Drinks – plc to entrepreneur – which will hopefully encourage lots of companies and businesses throughout the UK to establish new and exciting partnerships with charities.

The French philosopher and mathematician Blaise Pascal once wrote to a correspondent: 'I have made this letter longer than usual, only because I have not had the time to make it shorter.' Good man! I have endeavoured to keep this book short and concise and as simple as possible. My aim is to encourage and provoke, to drop the proverbial pebble in the water and watch while the ripples spread outwards. I want to start a conversation in your mind, a debate in your social circle and in your workplace, about the importance of giving – to your family and friends, to those less fortunate than yourself, to the environment or the arts, for instance – and to show you how giving to others will truly enrich your own life.

As Winston Churchill said: 'We make a living by what we get but we make a life by what we give.'

Introduction

SERENDIPITY

'Who is up for running the London Marathon?'

It was 1988 and I was at a Christmas party. Our host had managed to get hold of twelve entries for the race from one of the sponsors.

Feeling very much at peace with the world after several glasses of wine, I put my hand up. Then I went home and enthusiastically called an equally non-athletic friend, Ricky, a senior paediatrician at Great Ormond Street hospital, persuading him to join me in my latest adventure.

Christmas came and went, and with it the start of the New Year. On 18 January 1989, a date inscribed on my memory for ever, a fax arrived at my office, from the then athletics correspondent of the *Sunday Times*. His message was simple and to the point: 'You have twelve weeks until the London Marathon. Here is a "get you round somehow" training schedule. You need to start running.'

That night, I poured myself a stiff gin and tonic and considered my situation. My bluff had been called. Forty years old, a couple of stone overweight and very unfit (despite being the owner of two successful bicycle shops), I had foolishly volunteered to run 26.2 miles.

A couple of my wife's business colleagues were having dinner with us that night, and, as I described my plight, they immediately offered to donate £1,000 to a charity of my choice if I made it across the finishing line.

I started training. Slowly.

The weeks passed. As race day drew closer I decided that if I was going to go through all this pain and suffering I might as well do it for something worthwhile. Like many others I was vaguely aware of the world of charities, had even thought that it would be good to support one, but never actually got round to it. I remembered then something that had happened a few years previously.

A young girl in a powered wheelchair had driven into the shop I owned in Covent Garden. She pressed a control that raised her seat until she was the same height as the counter, bought an item, lowered the seat, then sped out into the piazza. I was intrigued enough to remember the name of the manufacturers and called them to discover that each wheelchair cost £3,500.

I asked if they had any children on their waiting list. They mentioned a girl called Sammy who had cerebral palsy and lived in Lincoln. As much to give myself courage and inspiration for the marathon ahead, I cleared a day from my diary, got on a train and went to meet her.

Sammy and her grandmother met me at the station and took me home to tea. I had never met a disabled child and I had no idea what cerebral palsy was. I spent about two hours talking to them both and was profoundly moved. Sammy was very bright, but had trouble with her speech and was unable to move much without help from her granny or a friend. I asked Sammy for a picture of herself and returned to London, where I reported back to Ricky. We agreed to run for Sammy, to buy her a powered wheelchair.

INTRODUCTION

We sent begging letters to all our friends with a picture of Sammy and the message: 'We are going to do something daft and mildly heroic, to run 26.2 miles to help a young girl who can't move herself about independently to get out of her front door on her own.'

By the day of the London Marathon, neither of us had run more than 6 miles, but we had raised over £9,000, an extraordinary sum in those days. Some people even sponsored us to cross the starting line! Ricky, who had been expressly told by his doctor not to run because of a medical condition but had got himself signed off as fit anyway, put a large X on his number (to identify himself to First Aid stations) and strapped some pills to his wrist. We hugged each other and exclaimed, 'All for one and one for all!' Then we set off into the unknown, with almost no idea of what we were doing. We knew it was going to be 'a little' challenging but, we reasoned, we had all day to reach the finish.

Six hours and thirty minutes later, when all the traffic separation schemes had been removed, I crossed the finishing line! Ricky had made it in a more respectable five hours. Our mission had been accomplished. We headed home for a hot bath, and then out for a great celebratory dinner with our wives, Shuna and Sarah, overjoyed and knackered and proudly wearing our medals.

Suddenly a door had been opened. Everyone wanted to help Sammy. What about the many more children who needed such equipment? we were asked. Surely there was a charity that specialised in providing it?

But there wasn't. With no knowledge of the charity world, and even less idea of how to start a charity, Ricky,

Shuna and I began to explore the possibility of creating an organisation to encourage other people to do what we had done.

A successful business friend offered us £5,000 to fund the start-up costs; another who had considerable charity experience offered to help register ours. We hosted a lunch for senior figures in the world of disability at The Institute of Child Health to see if there was a need for a new charity specialising in mobility. They unanimously gave their blessing and support.

Six months later we had cajoled nine friends to run the New York Marathon in November. Between us we raised £45,000. My wife Shuna had inspirationally thought up the name Whizz-Kidz and found a free desk in her office, as the phone started ringing and wheelchairs needed to be ordered for new children. Another friend, Lorraine, with eight years experience in Harley Street, offered to help part-time.

In April 1990, just one year after the London Marathon, Whizz-Kidz became a registered charity. Since then it has been nominated as Blue Peter's charity, and been the official charity for the Flora London Marathon. In 2006 Whizz-Kidz became Tesco's charity of the year and their partnership set a new record, raising an amazing £3.4 million. These are major landmarks for a comparatively small charity. It has now raised over £40 million, provided mobility equipment for over 4,500 disabled children and helped thousands more. It has become well-respected throughout the UK and is the largest supplier of paediatric mobility aids outside the National Health Service. Many of the best people on the planet have worked at and with Whizz-Kidz over the years, and still do. Bright, energetic, committed and fun people, who have all left their own imprint on the growth of the organisation.

The Rewards of Giving

The improvement in mobility helped to make Sammy's life a little better – and it completely changed mine. I began to learn first hand about the impact and rewards of 'giving'. I realised that people who give, who go out of their way to help others, often get as much as they give back in return.

I have 'persuaded' thousands of people to run marathons, climb mountains, create events, and to adopt Whizz-Kidz as their company's charity of the year. And I myself have run more marathons, led overseas treks, attended hundreds of events, and watched people taking part, having fun and sometimes raising huge amounts of money.

I have noticed that when many of these people meet a disabled young person, often the child for whom they had raised the money, the impact on them can be enormous. They are both moved and humbled that their fundraising efforts have helped a child who was unable to move, move. To become independently mobile, to 'whizz' about on their own, go shopping, go to a decent school, play with friends, take part in sport. Not infrequently people confide in me that helping a child move has been the best thing they had done in the year.

I have discovered what an enormous privilege it is to be able to help others and how hugely rewarding it is to be able to inspire all kinds of other people to do so. In addition, I have met some of the loveliest families you could ever wish to meet. And, of course, lots of perfectly horrible

INTRODUCTION

children – especially you lot who were on the Kidz Boards, you know who you are!

Ricky, Shuna and myself simply feel very blessed, that we were just the right people in the right place at the right time. True serendipity.

To end with a story:

One day I visited a school in Edinburgh and was introduced to a young man called Shaun. He was blind and had cerebral palsy – so he couldn't see, or move about independently. He was asked to show me how his new powered wheelchair worked, so he set off on his own round the school – the wheelchair had a laser on the bottom that followed a track from his classroom to the dining room – and arrived back to much applause from his friends. On the way out his physiotherapist thanked Whizz-Kidz and myself for helping to change Shaun's life. Then she said, softly, that it had taken her two years to show him how to manage the wheelchair's controls. She gave me a hug and left. And I just sat in my car alone, crying. And deeply humbled.

→ www.whizz-kidz.org.uk

Chapter 1

WHY GIVING IS GOOD FOR YOU

'You will find that the mere resolve not to be useless, and the honest desire to help other people, will, in the quickest and delicatest of ways, improve yourself.'

John Ruskin

You've tried everything to improve yourself and become a better you. You've dieted, given up smoking, abandoned booze, joined a gym and read (with mild incredulity) a couple of 'how to be outstanding at sex' books. You've studied time management (but still can't get the most important things done), absorbed all the latest tomes on leadership and empowerment (but *still* people argue with you), or how to be 'positive' and eliminate your fears and insecurities, or how to become a millionaire (which you're not).

After an initial burst of genuine commitment and enthusiasm, the new forward-thinking, improved and highly disciplined you has . . . well, flagged. Things have somehow slipped. You are not noticeably fitter, thinner, sexier, richer or even more effective. You know that if you keep doing the same things you'll keep getting the same results, but now you've become despondent. Downhearted by your own lack of self-discipline, staying power and inability to get better at anything, you are carrying on as before.

Well, I have good news for you. This book is completely different. By reading it you can improve your own life. Enormously.

It really is true that the more you give – of yourself, your thoughts, your time and your money – to people less fortunate than yourself, and to people who are experiencing difficult times, the more you will receive in the form of discovering a purpose, new friendships, love, learning and a large topping-up of your human spirit.

This book is about charity and giving, but it is also a self-help book. You will help yourself by going out of your way to help others. If you follow even a couple of the paths and ideas in this book, you will transform not only your own life, but those of your friends and your family, as well as the many people you don't yet know.

Giving reaches right into the very best part of you. Everyone has so much to give, whatever their position or state of mind. Ultimately, what makes us happy is being able to empathise with others and to receive that empathy in return. The work you do for others will become one of the best parts of you.

What is the Point of You?

Are you in a rut? Are you plodding through life, bored out of your mind, at a dull and predictable pace? Or are you tearing around, unbelievably busy but with hardly any time to do the things you really do want to, and at the same time feeling unfulfilled, discontented and plain knackered? You have officially 'made it', but still ... 'There has to be more to life,' you cry.

Of course there is more to life. You do have a special purpose to fulfil in this world. Every one of us is unique. We all have a great opportunity to leave the world a better place than when we arrived. We are alive for such a short while, perhaps seventy years, and much of this time is spent simply learning about life, and how to navigate our way through it. Working, sleeping and eating. Week by week, year by year. But we need to carve out some time to leave our own fingerprint on the world, before our life is used up. We must just take a moment to slow down, to press the pause button and think.

Some management experts and lifestyle gurus suggest that you do the 'funeral exercise'. In this you imagine your own funeral. Everyone you know is there, talking about you, swapping stories and remembrances. One or two members of your family, and perhaps a best friend, make speeches about you. What would they all be saying? What would they all remember you for?

When your time is up, what will have been your contribution? How will you have used the 'gift of life'? The answer will be important to you at the end of your life, so it really is worth asking the question now. The saying 'No one ever said on their deathbed that they wish they'd spent more time at the office' is slightly glib, but true. The deal done or missed, the salary or promotion won or lost will not really matter. But you *will* wish that you had spent more time with your family and friends, or made up that quarrel, or taken the risk and done something you had always wanted to do which you put off because your courage failed, or because there wasn't enough time. You will wish that you had left the world a little bit better off for your presence, and probably feel rather sad, if not 'terminally' depressed, if you haven't.

Many writers and academics have pressed upon us the idea that personal happiness and contentment in life are not linked to money and material possessions, but to having a sense of true purpose. There is a remarkable and powerful book, *Man's Search for Meaning*, written by a man called Viktor Frankl, who endured several years in Nazi death camps. His father, mother, brother and wife died in the camps or the gas chambers, leaving only himself and his sister alive. He experienced hunger, cold and brutality, and hourly expected death. Frankl noticed that, amidst the appalling misery, most prisoners simply gave up, but a few managed to survive the most terrible ordeals. They were the ones who had the strongest reason for living, a purpose in life. Fond of quoting Nietzsche – 'He who has a "why" to live can bear almost any "how"' – Frankl developed the theory and practice of 'logotherapy', man's search for meaning as the primary motivational force in his life: 'This meaning is unique and specific in that it must be fulfilled by him alone; only then does it achieve a significance which will satisfy his own *will* to meaning.'

Then there is Abraham Maslow, a renowned psychologist and inspirational figure in 'personality theories', who created his famous 'hierarchy of needs', which organised human needs into three broad levels: physiological (food, water, a roof over your head); psychological (love, self-esteem, safety and a sense of belonging); and self-actualisation (the ability to make the best use of your talents, personality and capabilities). Self-actualisers are always striving to develop and express themselves. Once we have met our basic needs we begin wanting to be useful, to have meaning.

Success to Significance

Many people become successful in their chosen way of life, in business and industry, the arts, the media, sport, teaching, the academic world, medicine. In fact, thank goodness, in every area of life, people become very good at what they do: taxi drivers, vicars, gardeners, builders, charity workers, fishermen, farmers, retailers, journalists and writers – if I haven't mentioned your world, forgive me, but I hope I have made the point. People work hard, succeed at many different levels and are usually rewarded in a suitable fashion. Or paid the rate for the job, at least.

But are they or you **significant?** This does not mean giving it all up to help out in a local drug rehabilitation unit. It's about living a useful life, recognising how fortunate you are and using your resources to help others, and being worthwhile. We can all think of people we know who have either had, or who continue to have, a positive influence on our lives, and those of others around them. They are the significant ones, the people who leave their thumbprint on the world.

Others miss the point of life, fail to be remotely useful to anyone, and remain in their own world, always busy and completely caught up with their own ambitions, problems and desires. If they do help people at all it's as an afterthought – a hastily scribbled cheque. But they never really seem to be happy or at peace.

Stephen Covey, and Roger and Rebecca Merrill's book, *First Things First,* identifies our core needs as: to live, to love, to learn and to leave a legacy.

To live is to take care of our physical need of food, shelter and clothing.

To love is to recognise our social need to love and be loved, and to relate to others.

To learn is to realise our mental need to develop and grow.

To leave a legacy is to acknowledge our spiritual need to have a sense of purpose, personal consequence and contribution.

We have to perfect the first three needs simply in order to navigate our way through life, but to experience a life truly worth living we must leave a legacy.

'How Much Land Does a Man Need?'

In 1886, the Russian novelist Tolstoy published a short story about greed and ambition called 'How Much Land Does a Man Need?' The story goes like this:

A woman and her husband, who live in town, go to visit the woman's younger sister and her husband, who run a small farm in the country. The two women argue about the merits of each of their worlds – the style of town life versus the honest simplicity of living in the country. The conversation unsettles the farmer, whose name is Pakhom, and he develops a desire to have more land. Then, he reasons, they would have more money and their problems would disappear.

One day a merchant is passing through the village and stops at Pakhom's house. He has just returned from the land of the Bashkirs, where he has bought 13,000 acres of land for 1,000 roubles. 'There is so much land that you couldn't walk round it in a year,' he says. 'It all belongs to the Bashkirs. Yes the people there are as stupid as sheep, and you can get land off them for practically nothing.'

WHY GIVING IS GOOD FOR YOU

Pakhom is very excited and sets off to find this magical kingdom. He discovers the Bashkirs living by a river, leading a very simple and happy life. They greet Pakhom, and give him food and drink, while he gives them presents in return. He tells them that he has heard they have much land, and that it's much better than his overcrowded plot. Their elder agrees that Pakhom can have as much land as he likes, as they have plenty of it. Pakhom asks the price and the elder replies: 'We have a set price - a thousand roubles a day. However much as you can walk round in one day will be yours. But there is one condition: if you don't return on the same day to the spot where you started, your money is lost.'

The following morning Pakhom goes with the villagers to the top of a small hill. The elder tells him that all the land he can see is theirs, and he can have any part he wants. Pakhom puts his 1,000 roubles into the elder's hat and sets off with a spade to mark his boundaries. After several hours in the very hot sun he starts to tire, but he keeps going. An hour to suffer, a lifetime to live, he thinks, and takes a detour to include a particularly good hollow where flax would grow well. Then, as he heads back to the hillock and the villagers, he sees the sun begin to sink. Exhausted by the heat, he realises that he has gone too far and starts to worry that he will be late. He throws off his coat, his boots, his flask and his cap and starts running toward the hill, his heart beating like a hammer, his mouth parched and his lungs burning. In desperation he reaches the hill just as the sun sets. He runs up it to find the elder at the top, laughing 'Ah that's a fine fellow,' the elder says. 'He has gained much land!'

And with that, Pakhom's legs give way and he falls to the

ground. He dies of exhaustion.

Pakhom's servant digs a grave for him. Six feet from his head to his heels was all he needed.

Enough?

Which brings us nicely to the issue of Enough. What is enough? It is a big question because deciding how much you actually *need* to live a satisfactory and happy life marks a turning point in your personal maturity. A small but important step towards growing up and becoming useful.

However well you have done in your career, however hard you have worked to become a success, however much money you have made, at some point you have to pause and say: 'Enough. I have enough.' And of course, you know as well as I do that enough is never enough. Earning more and more money is a game without end.

How many cars, houses, sets of clothes, holidays can you have before you lose the will to live? And when you have got all this, what are you going to do?

So, how much money do you need to live a happy and contented life? *Really* need. This is not necessarily the same as your current expenditure plans. Or even what you have programmed yourself to believe that you must have. It's an important question for several reasons, not least because the more you want, the more you are actually going to have to earn, and the harder you will have to work.

Of course, the answer to the question is less than you think. We all need a roof over our heads, food to nourish us, friends to support us and make us laugh, companionship, a purpose in life, some faith and very little else.

Some years ago I asked a Yorkshire businessman why

he didn't expand his successful and profitable business. He replied with striking simplicity: 'You can only sleep in one bed each night, eat three meals a day at the most and drive one car at a time.'

When we have reached our own personal base camp and achieved our needs and goals, most of us settle contently into life, our comfort zone. There is very little more that will impact on the way we choose to live.

> *Often people attempt to live their lives backwards. They try to have more things, or more money, in order to have more of what they want so that they will be happier ... The way it actually works is the reverse. You must first be who you are, then do what you need to do, in order to get what you want.* Margaret Young

More money, a higher salary, a better job with more power, a better and bigger house in a nicer area, a smarter or faster car, more expensive meals, exotic holidays; more stylish clothes, a boat, a plane – and seconds of each. Is this just greed? Is it insecurity? Is it the power of advertising? Is it the need to keep up with friends or neighbours, or impress members of our own family? Is it straightforward shallowness? Who really knows?

Professor Northcote Parkinson wrote a famous book called 'Parkinson's Law'. In it he put forward a very simple proposition: 'Work expands to fill the time available for its completion.' In other words, people usually take all the time allotted – and often more – to accomplish any particular task. There is a spending equivalent, created solely for the purpose of this book, which I have called 'Michael's Law': 'Your spending is likely to expand to the level of your earnings – and often exceed them, however much you earn.' Look at it another way. If you gave away a small percentage of what you earned to others who are less fortunate than yourselves, would you miss it? Really miss it? I know of an extraordinarily successful businessman, who worked out when he was young how much money he would need to earn to live a comfortable life for ever. He then devised a plan to earn that amount of money – and to give everything else away. Which is exactly what he did, and he is now a major charitable donor and venture philanthropist. He makes large sums of money to give away, because he has already decided in his own mind and heart what is enough.

You will die as you entered the world – with nothing. Obvious though it may seem, you cannot take any of your valued possessions with you. You can leave your money or assets to your family, your friends or a good cause, but those left behind are more likely to remember your human spirit than your money, in the form of friendships made, people helped, good enterprises created, laughter caused and values upheld.

Some years ago I sat down with my wife to work out what was enough for us. To cover the costs of our mortgage, our children's education, our living expenses and our slightly feeble pensions arrangements.

About the same time I met Charles Handy, the well-known management guru and writer, who first developed the concept of living a portfolio life, and wrote about it in his book *The Elephant and the Flea*. Now I try to emulate the work plan that he practises with his wife Elizabeth.

I split my working life into three. One-third of it I use to advise companies and individuals about how to give effectively, and I charge for this work. This is how I earn a living. One-third of my time I research and learn and write about charities and philanthropy. This hugely informs my ability to advise people, and is a fascinating and often humbling experience. The final third of my time I spend doing pro bono work – helping a friend's colleague to manage a charity, or lending a hand in my local church and community. It is all hugely rewarding.

You might be thinking, 'That seems a good way to live but it's all very well for him ...'

But the important point is that I can only divide my time like this because Shuna and I have worked out what is enough for ourselves and our family. I can tell you it is very liberating! BUT! It only works if you have covered your own costs first. I could easily spend my whole life doing pro bono work while avoiding the issue of earning a living.

The Golden Rule

'Do unto others as you would have them do unto you.' These fourteen words from the Bible (Matthew, ch7, v12) sum up the leading moral philosophy in the world, one shared by all faiths and generally understood as the key moral code of behaviour.

You should make the effort to treat everyone you know or meet as you would like to be treated. You want to mix with others, be treated fairly and behave in a way that allows you to be respected in return and helped when you are down. So do your family, friends, colleagues and everyone else. It is not an easy task to fulfil but there is really no excuse for not trying to behave as well as you possibly can towards others while you are in this world. Like forgiveness – see page 50 – it is quite simply a matter of personal choice. You can choose to behave well towards others or do nothing because you're too self-absorbed, or treat people badly. It really is that simple and that clear.

Beating people up – verbally, mentally or physically, in business or in your private life – is unacceptable. People don't like such behaviour, and neither do they trust people who bully others to get their own way. Gossiping or lying about others is horrible, pride is tedious, arrogance irritating, promiscuity damaging.

There are any number of real, imagined or psychological reasons why people behave badly. We all do to a greater or lesser extent, but we should and can try to behave towards others as we would like them to behave towards us.

Having Faith

You may think that we live in a faithless world, where the majority don't believe in a god or go to church. But you are wrong. There are roughly 6.6 billion people in the world, and of these more than 2 billion are Christian, 1.3 billion Muslim, 800 million Hindu and 500 million Buddhist, not to mention numerous other religions and faiths.

All of these people have a spiritual life and believe in a God – a higher being who created the world in which we live and who answers prayers – or in another spiritual life. Each of these religions and faiths has withstood the test of time. They have been followed and practised for several thousand years, as well as questioned, debated and misinterpreted. Their teachings and beliefs provide the moral framework for every society in the world. All stress the importance of helping the less fortunate members of their societies, and place great emphasis on giving both money and love, quietly and with humility.

Jesus's teaching in the Sermon on the Mount (Matthew, chs 5, 6 and 7) and the parables are the foundations of British law and social attitudes. And Paul's second letter to the Corinthians tells us that 'Whoever sows sparingly will also reap sparingly, and whoever sows generously will reap generously.'

In Judaism, *tzedakah* (literally 'righteousness') is more than charity. The word's root is related to justice. Helping others is the just, the right thing to do, and the obligation of *tzedakah* rests on everyone, rich and poor alike.

One of the most important principles of Islam is that all things belong to God, and that wealth is held by human beings in trust. One of the five pillars of Islam is *zakat*, which means both 'purification' and 'growth'. Our possessions must be purified by setting aside a proportion for those in need, and this cutting back balances us and encourages new growth. For most Muslims, this involves a payment each year of 2.5 per cent of one's capital.

Then there is prayer. If you ask your friends and colleagues, you will discover that most people have prayed at some time during their life, if only when life has been tough.

Even if you are not a religious person, a period of quiet reflection at the start and or the end of each day, just 'talking to yourself' about life, being grateful, or meditating is a calming and positive thing to do.

I 'discovered' real prayer in middle age, and am constantly surprised by how many times my prayers are answered. Faith is personal, of course, but I try to start each day with a quiet period of prayer and Bible reading. I pray for guidance in the day ahead, for the decisions I have to take, for my hopes and dreams, for members of my family and friends. Like any other working life, some mornings are great, full of insight and peace. Other times I can't settle and rush off to work. Then, before I go to bed, I thank God for all the events of the day. This simple act always gives me enormous peace and a sense of proportion. It is a special time.

Why Should You Bother?

This universal moral code works because each individual needs help, love and care. <u>Everyone</u> you know is insecure, and I've underlined <u>everyone</u> to emphasise the point. I am always amazed by how many people haven't really grasped this. It may seem to you as if everyone else is a tremendous success in their chosen job, has the most exciting social life imaginable, can afford whatever they want, is wonderfully happy with their partner, and is the best parent on the planet. And if they do have a problem in one area of their life – which they might quietly confide to you one day over a coffee – well, the rest of their life is a ball.

Of course, this is nonsense.

Some people are better at handling their anxieties than others, but never all of them. Others are better at dealing with or covering up their problems. Certain problems may appear small to you, either because you don't share or understand it. Or you have cracked it, and moved on.

But most of us spend a considerable part of our lives trying to resolve our very real problems on our own. And the more serious the problem, the more insecure we become

WHY GIVING IS GOOD FOR YOU

about it, and the more reluctant to discuss it. It is our insecurity that stops us asking for help.

When we do take action to deal with our fears, it can very often transform our lives. People actually want to help if only we would ask them. It is a great relief to find that somebody shares our woes. And there is nothing more powerful than discovering that a really knotty problem we are fighting has been experienced and conquered by someone else.

Sometimes just sharing a problem with someone who is happy to listen is therapy enough and of immense value. It helps to clear your mind and speed up your decision-making process. A knowledgeable friend or colleague might recommend a new job opportunity, counsellor, back pain specialist, gym or accountant, for example.

How you spend your working day, what you do and who you work with are all sources of angst. That's if you have a job at all. Are you in the right job to maximise your talents and make you a happy bunny, or are you locked in the working-to-pay-the-rent-or-mortgage syndrome? Do you think you are earning enough money? Are you enjoying your job? Is your company or organisation a good place to work? If you wanted to progress in it, would it be possible, or even a good idea? We spend a great deal of life working, and it uses up a lot of time, energy and talent. So it needs to be enjoyable and worthwhile. Many books have been published about how to discover the real you and find a new career. One of the very best is *What Colour is Your Parachute?* by Richard Nelson Bolles. If work is an issue that concerns you, buy the book and do the exercises.

And what about the rest of your life? Do you have enough time to be with your wife, husband, children, parents or close friends, to do charitable work, help out in the community, pursue a hobby, or to be a useful member of the local rugby, football or cricket club? Put simply – do you have a life outside work?

We have to relate to and with others every day. Daniel Goleman's remarkable book, *Emotional Intelligence*, should be on the secondary school syllabus. In it he argues that your Emotional Intelligence (EQ) is more important to your future happiness and success in life that your IQ. In other words, your ability to exercise self-control, to empathise with others, together with your persistence not to give up when things get tough and your ability to motivate yourself, are of paramount importance. He suggests that as much as 70 per cent of your future happiness and success depends on your ability to understand and harness emotional skills in yourself and others. It is certainly true that of all the things that we set out to do and achieve in life, a great chunk of our success lies in our ability to build a rapport with people. Empathy, understanding another person's point of view, is central to being liked, accepted and getting on.

It is a hugely difficult exercise, not least because we tend to look upon people and day-to-day problems from our own often very limited perspective, and make a judgment based on too little knowledge or understanding of a particular person's problems.

An Exercise

I want you to take a few moments to think of your three best friends. People you really like, know well and feel you could rely on if something dire happened. Write their

WHY GIVING IS GOOD FOR YOU

names down on a piece of paper.

I would like to suggest to you that they all have worries about their work, roles in life, finances or relationships, or concerns about their health, if not their own, then those of a close family member or friend.

So it naturally follows that if they are anxious about one or more aspect of life, then so is everyone else you know. In offices, in shops; politicians, high-powered business people, athletes, actors, comedians, *everyone*. They need help and support. And you need help and support. You are worried, anxious, insecure, full of questionable habits and strange little ways. So is everyone else.

What impact does this very simple thought have on you?

You Have Lots to be Grateful For

Some of us spend such a lot of time moaning about our lot that we forget to be grateful for all the good things we have. We focus on things we don't or can't have, the things that won't go right. We become secretly envious of other people's supposed good fortune, their families, friendships, finances and even fitness.

It really is good to count our blessings, and to be grateful for them. I remember one particularly difficult period at Whizz-Kidz, when it seemed to me that everyone associated with the charity had decided to behave badly at the same time, some of them not entirely without cause. I was feeling particularly down when one of the trustees rang up to ask how things were going. When I told him, he said in a very exasperated manner, 'Why is everyone whinging? The children have much more difficult lives and they never complain.'

It was one of those 'a-ha' moments in which I realised that, during my whole career at Whizz-Kidz, I had never met a disabled child who complained. They were all upbeat and positive, wanting to get on with their lives and contribute as much as they could to the charity. Despite their discomfort and, often, pain, the difficulties they had in getting about, gaining entry into a proper education, developing a social life and with it acceptance from their peers, they were up for anything.

Being grateful is an attitude of mind, and a vital one. Only when you settle down and give thanks for the blessings that you have can you become balanced sufficiently to think of giving to others.

Make a list now of all the things and people that you are grateful for. It will take you to some surprising places and may make you smile.

Serving

Serving means being unconditionally committed to the growth, success and well-being of others without expecting thanks, praise or reward.

We all need people to support and encourage us, to show interest in our lives and adventures, to cheer our successes, and to comfort us when we are down, and to forgive us when we make mistakes (as we all do).

I love it when people give their time to help me sort out a problem, show me kindness, make an effort to understand my point of view or situation, hug me physically or mentally. Especially when I have made a Horlicks of something, or not done what I said I would, when I said I would. And I love doing the same for them.

In 1970, Robert Greenleaf wrote an article called 'The Servant as Leader', and has since developed and taught the idea of servant leadership in businesses and communities. Inspired by a 1932 Hermann Hesse story, 'Journey to the East', Greenleaf argued that those who want to lead must first learn to serve.

'Journey to the East' is a fictional account of a mystical organisation called the League which embarks on a voyage with its variety of members, among them artists, musicians and poets. One of the quieter members was a man known only as Leo, a servant. He helped to carry the luggage and was often assigned to the personal service of the speaker (the group's acknowledged leader). This unaffected man had something so pleasing, so unobtrusively winning about him that everyone loved him. He did his work gaily, usually sang or whistled as he went along, was never seen except when needed – in fact, an ideal servant.

One day Leo suddenly disappeared. For Hermann, and for the whole travelling troupe, the departure of Leo had dire results. Faith began to diminish, dissention destroyed the peaceful unity the group had enjoyed from the beginning. It seemed that when Leo left, with him went the prosperity of the League and the cohesion of the whole group of travellers. It wasn't long before the author deserted the journey.

Ten years later, he found himself in a certain city, trying to fulfil his long-standing goal to write a history of the League, only to discover that Leo, the humble servant, was actually the League's president.

There is a Great Deal to Do

It is time to step on to the pitch rather than continue to watch from the stands. There is more than enough for *you* to do in the world to alleviate poverty, literally save lives (plural), the planet (singular, we only have one), or just provide a shoulder for someone to rest their head on, a hug for a friend in need. To paraphrase an old First World War poster: 'Your World Needs YOU!' And all your friends and family.

Global poverty is not only shocking of itself, and a complete affront to those of us in the mainly Western world who claim to be civilised, *but it can be eradicated.* We have the knowledge, the resources and the financial wealth to save and improve the lives of the 1 billion poorest people on the planet. It would cost comparatively little – especially compared with, say, the amount nations spend on arms and wars. We simply lack the will. In effect, we – that is, you and I – are letting these people suffer and die when they needn't. Real people.

Put another way, 20,000 people die unnecessarily each day, the equivalent of the population of Stratford-upon-Avon. For a glimpse of the reality of global poverty try reading *The End of Poverty: Economic Possibilities for Our Time* by Jeffrey Sachs.

A similar argument goes for the terrible threat to the planet we are living on. We know that the way we live currently is not sustainable, that the population is likely to rise from 6.6 billion to 9 billion by 2050, that it is going to be fearfully hard to feed all these people and we are going to run out of resources like oil, and even water in many areas. As Lester Brown has written, if we do not do something about it now, our children are going to ask us, quite justifiably, why we didn't act. (See page 111–115.)

Very small sums of money are needed to help the poorest people on the planet. Earlier this year I spent some time in Southern India and visited several orphanages – full of sparkling, hopeful young people, mostly girls. To provide each child with a home, to clothe and feed and provide them with education for a year costs £150. One hundred children can receive care and love and an education, be lifted out of poverty and given a better future for £15,000 a year. It costs £250 a year to pay for a teacher.

In Africa 50p will provide a mosquito net to protect a child against malaria. But they haven't got 50p. The expression 'living on $1 a day or less' is too glib by far: people living in such poverty do not *have* a dollar to spend; there is no dollar in sight; they are living in a non-cash economy. At least a billion individuals are struggling for survival, people who are denied access to the most basic needs to keep them alive: food, water, medicine.

Poverty is relative, of course. But deep, unremitting poverty also exists in Britain and indeed America. The recent Unicef report into child poverty in twenty-one wealthy countries placed the United Kingdom in last place. The six dimensions they measured were: material well-being; health and safety; educational well-being; family and peer relationships; behaviours and risk; and subjective well-being. In every area our children get a raw deal. The Scandinavian countries take the top four positions in the table – and surprise, surprise – these are countries where tax paid is amongst the highest in the world, and where many polls also put them top of the 'happiness leagues'. Coincidence?

According to Oxfam, just under 1 in 4 people in the UK

– or nearly 13 million – live in poverty. This includes nearly 1 in 3 children (almost 4 million). These people have simply been left behind. It is a root cause of the rise in violence, drugs and gang culture as a way out of a life that doesn't seem worth living. To compare levels of UK poverty with those in Africa is not a fruitful exercise and misses the point. Which is that in a supposedly civilised and wealthy country, a quarter of the population struggle to find proper housing, essential clothing and regular meals, and constantly juggle bills and debt.

Even today, supposedly well-educated and intelligent people will still insist that there are no really poor people in Britain. In pubs and at dinner all over the country, the ill-informed actively dismiss the poor, the disabled, the mentally ill, the addicted, the homeless, the jobless and the troublesome young. Everyone 'should pull themselves together' and 'get a job'. Some people just need to get out more!

Whether it is the life of an orphan in India or Africa; or the life of a friend going through treatment for breast cancer; or caring for someone who is elderly and infirm; or helping a young person to improve their education and self-esteem; or saving the planet single-handedly by buying energy-saving lightbulbs; there is lots to do.

As the sports shoe manufacturer Nike used to say: Just Do It.

A Blessing

If you woke up this morning with more health than illness, you are more blessed than the one million people who will not survive this week.

If you have never experienced the danger of battle, the loneliness of imprisonment, the agony of torture or the pangs of starvation, you are ahead of 500 million other people in the world.

If you can attend church without fear of harassment, arrest, torture or death, you are more blessed than 3 billion people in the world today.

If you have food in the fridge, clothes on your back, a roof over your head and a place to sleep, you are richer than 70 per cent of the world's population.

If you have money in the bank, in your wallet and some spare change in a dish at home, you are also among the top 8 per cent of the world's wealthiest people.

If you hold up your head with a smile on your face and are truly thankful to God, you are blessed because the majority can but most do not.

If you can hold someone's hand, hug him or her, or even touch them on the shoulder, you are blessed because you offer love through your touch.

If you hear this message, you have now received a blessing from God. You can't say blessings don't come your way.

Chapter 2

CHARITY BEGINS AT HOME

'That best portion of a good man's life, his little nameless, unremembered acts of kindness and of love.'

William Wordsworth

So, you've decided to take action, to give more and to look for opportunities to help other people and causes.

Congratulations! Setting aside a part of your life for helping others will be hugely rewarding, sometimes challenging and often great fun. You are about to become a significant and powerful force for good. To leave a legacy.

Probably best of all, you will find a sense of purpose that will provide proportion and balance against all the struggles and difficulties in life. You won't become a saint overnight, or get mentioned in the New Year's Honours list (well, you might one day!), but in deciding to help others you will change and enhance both your life and the lives of those others, for many years ahead. Literally. Isn't that an amazing thought?

You must start quietly, and learn as you go along. As you become older, wiser and gentler, and do more for others, the satisfaction and reward you receive will become an increasingly important part of your life.

CHARITY BEGINS AT HOME

> *" What we think, or what we know, or what we believe is in the end of little consequence; the only consequence is what we do. "* John Ruskin

People often think about doing something useful; they know that they want to help other people, to do something worthwhile with their lives. They talk about it a great deal but somehow they never get round to it. 'One day, when I've got more time . . .' they say. But the time to start giving and being useful is *now*, not tomorrow. The plain truth is that you have absolutely no guarantee of a tomorrow. Your own circumstances may change, other people's problems could get worse while you are 'really busy'; they might even die suddenly. You might! Children grow up, change and fly away surprisingly quickly. The opportunity to help particular people, special friends and others who need your help might vanish completely, while you are 'thinking about it' or 'waiting for more time'.

Perfection, procrastination, paralysis. In order to do something **perfectly**, or even just the best we can do, we **procrastinate**, waiting for a better time. And grind to a halt. **Paralysis**. All our good thoughts and intentions come to nought and nothing useful gets done at all. Don't worry about being perfect; do it anyway.

Thinking about doing something for other people, knowing that you could or should, and believing that everyone else should do so is of little use unless you actually rise up and do something. How many times have you heard people say that they wish they had a purpose in life and want to 'put something back'? I have met many, including lots of people applying for jobs at Whizz-Kidz. Some even genuinely meant it.

This is a personal wake-up call to those of you who feel that there must be more to life. There is! You should be doing something useful to help other people. With just a little effort and commitment you can. And it will improve your life tremendously.

It's time to engage your gentle, caring side. To show love, kindness, thoughtfulness and empathy. The best part of you, the real you that perhaps spends too much time buried beneath the hustle, stress and problems of everyday life. The part that is moved by music, cries during soppy films, loves good friends and is actually touched by the plight of others in this country and around the world. As the Dalai Lama said: 'If you want to be happy, practise compassion. If you want others to be happy, practise compassion.'

Making a Difference to People You Know

Helping other people must start with those who are closest to you: your family, your friends, your colleagues at work as well as those on the outer circle of your world. Your actions and behaviour have an influence on all these people on a regular basis, so before we start our 'out-reach' to other vulnerable people in society we need to pause for a moment, and reflect that we already know many of them personally. And they need help. I call this 'in-reach'.

Step 1: How is Everybody?

I want you to set some time aside from your busy, stressful, fascinating, boring life to think about these people and their lives. Put a decent amount of time in your diary within the

CHARITY BEGINS AT HOME

next seven days. Try to make sure that you don't have to be somewhere, or do something for a couple of hours or so. Because this is just the beginning of what will turn out to be a really interesting, involving and positive experience.

Choose a quiet spot where you will not be interrupted by a phone – turn off your mobile – or by someone popping in to ask you something: a room at home; a favourite spot in a park or a field; a rug beneath a tree or beside a river; a bench looking out to sea; a quiet pub or library. Have with you a pad of paper, a pen, your address or telephone book to prompt ideas, and perhaps a can of drink, a bottle of water or even a glass or two of your favourite wine.

Your mission is to think about other people from *their* perspective. Try to imagine yourself in their shoes. This can be quite difficult, especially trying to override our opinions and judgements of other people, their behaviour and mannerisms.

How is everybody? It is quite extraordinary how focusing your mind on another person's life for five minutes will give you a new insight into their world and some of the situations they are facing. We are all so busy, and so concerned about our own lives, our own triumphs and concerns, that the problems of even our closest friends often pass us by completely.

Are they happy? Pretty content and on good form? Is it their birthday soon (and are you about to forget it?) or are they about to celebrate something? Are they going for a job interview or have they just started a new job; taken an important exam or just passed one; moved home or retired? Is it time to congratulate them on something or wish them good luck? Ring them, email them or write a quick note. Now!

Perhaps they are not very happy and rather stressed, or not very well physically. Are they facing serious challenges at work or having problems with a relationship? Are they lonely or having a difficult time financially? What sorts of problems are they facing?

They might even be depressed. One in six people in the UK will suffer from some form of mental illness. I suffered a very nasty attack of clinical depression in my mid-forties and fortunately, with some excellent medical help, exercise, prayer and wonderful support from all my family and friends, I made a complete recovery. By being quite open about it I suddenly found significant numbers of people who were fellow sufferers, most of whom had never dared to tell anyone who didn't need to know.

Remember: <u>everyone</u> is insecure, however confident they may seem.

Step 2: Your Action Plan

Start by listing some names down the left-hand side of the paper. Next to each name, make a note of some of their concerns or reasons to be cheerful. Now take some time to think:

- **What is the best thing that you can do to help this person?**
- **When are you going to do it?**
- **What could you *do* today, in the next few days, or when you next see them, that would help them in a practical way, or show that you care about them? Make a time now or you will put it off. Remember, it is the little things you do that really help. (See also pages 56–59.)**

CHARITY BEGINS AT HOME

Just to put this in context, the week I wrote this chapter, one good friend was involved in a serious court case, which could have seen him sent to prison. One of his friends was dying with cancer; another friend announced that his marriage was over after thirty years, which led to the postponement of his daughter's wedding; and the mother of one of my daughter's close friends discovered that her breast cancer had reoccurred. And her partner recently suffered a stroke. (She has since sadly died.) I am tempted to say that this is an abnormal week but I suspect that it probably isn't. It is just that I have had time to log on to other people's worlds.

Finally, put the action you have decided upon in the next column and the date you are going to do it in the final column.

NAME	CONCERN	ACTION	TIME/DATE
Emma	Engaged at last!	Celebration lunch	ASAP
Liz	Trouble with son	Ring for chat	Today
David	Unhappy with partner	Meet for drink	This week
Tina	Miserable job / lonely	Ask to supper	Next week
Mum	Just had operation	Visit for two days	Ring now to get date in diary

Helping Your Family

'Oh, do we have to?' you groan. Challenging this one, isn't it? Think about your mother, father, husband, wife, partner, sister, brother, relatives, in-laws. In an ideal world, our relationships with those closest to us would be the warmest and most loving. But you don't have to be a psychologist to realise that those we know best we often judge most harshly. We see their questionable habits, weaknesses and sometimes nasty little ways. As they do ours.

And, of course, the really depressing fact is that if you have a problem or a dispute with a member of your family – whatever the cause, whoever did what to whom and whoever was right or wrong – it is hard to forgive. We have all heard: 'I will never speak to him/her again.' My father wasn't really on speaking terms with his brother; my father-in-law had a similar situation with his brother. I don't think either set had a lot in common, but it did seem an awful waste.

A Few Words on Forgiveness

Forgiving IS giving. Forgiving people for things they have said or done (or things you *think* they have said or done) that have made you cross, or perhaps hurt you, is hugely difficult and takes great courage. It is even more difficult when they are not in a forgiving mood and you have to continue making the effort and keeping the door open. But there is a simple truth about forgiveness – it is an act of choice. You can choose to forgive someone for something they have done to you, or to someone close to you, and move on. Or refuse to forgive, and carry the mistrust or

CHARITY BEGINS AT HOME

hatred with you to your grave.

Making the choice to forgive is actually a 'no-brainer'. It is a decision between continuing bitterness and positive healing. Harbouring bitterness will eat away at the good parts of you and make you angry, miserable and depressed. And quite possibly not a very nice person to be around. Whereas the healing benefits of forgiveness, perhaps a personal relationship restored that once again becomes loving and fun, and the positive sense of life moving on can be enormous. A huge burden is lifted.

Most misunderstandings are caused by lack of thought and compassion, sometimes by gossip, and very often by just getting the wrong end of the stick or having the wrong information. A very wise friend of mine has a wonderful expression: 'It's the manner not the matter.' It is so often not 'the matter' being discussed that causes so much anger and hurt, but the way in which it which it has been handled or expressed, 'the manner'. (Incidentally, this is especially true in management.) You have to be 'strong to be gentle': strong, kind and humble enough to be vulnerable, to say sorry, to forgive and to risk getting mauled in the process.

Helping Your Friends

How are your friends? The really good friends you haven't seen for ages, but would love to catch up with again. The people who you know well, and those you would like to get to know better. Where are they? When did you last see them? Are they OK or do they need a hug?

Perhaps you hardly see the friends that you really like since they moved, got married or began a new job. Proper friendships, the people who have been through lots with you, who you care most about and in turn care most about you, are invaluable. Wasting time with a friend, swapping news and just being together for no particular purpose is a true blessing and part of what friendships are all about.

Maybe this is a time for a 'social cull', or at least time to focus on spending your spare time with people you actually like as opposed to being continuously sociable.

One of my friends used to divide her friends into 'day time' and 'night time' friends. It was her way of separating all those friendly, chatty people you meet during the day – at school or at work – from those you would actually like to spend more time getting to know, invite home for supper, a chat and a drink.

You could try your hand at Desert Island Friends. In the real game, Desert Island Discs, you are cast away on a desert island with the Bible, the complete works of Shakespeare, one luxury and your eight favourite pieces of music. In Desert Island Friends, instead of your eight favourite pieces of music, you can take eight friends with you, including family members. It can be a very sobering game.

Most people can't actually name eight, and many wouldn't take members of their own family.

Helping People at Work

You spend a great deal of time with your colleagues at work. Some are a laugh, others seem really friendly but you don't see much of them during the day; some you wouldn't trust further than you can throw them, others are hugely ambitious and don't have a life; some have been there for most of their adult lives and live for the weekends, or to pursue an eccentric hobby!

Grab an internal phone list. Go through it and think for a moment about your colleagues' lives and what you know of them. Perhaps go to lunch with someone you usually wouldn't, or have a drink with them after work. You will be pleasantly surprised by how often people's lives and interests 'outside work' will make them more approachable, fun and human. Management team-building games to help bonding are one thing; one-to-one communication with a colleague over a drink will probably do the trick as well.

Helping People You Hardly Know

We all tend to like people who are similar to ourselves, or whom we admire, and spend most of our time with them. There is nothing wrong with this, but for a while I would like you to think of the people that you don't know well, wouldn't normally socialise with, or even think of talking to – people who are quite simply on the edge of your social radar screen, those you might even think boring. (One definition of a drinks party is 'a gathering where everyone present is a crashing bore except you'.) My mother-in-law, a wonderful lady called Eleanor, always insisted that no one was boring if you asked them about themselves and then listened to them. I would tell her that a particular person was as dull as ditchwater, but I soon learned that she was completely right. No one is boring if you persevere.

People's most interesting subject is themselves. Ask them about their family, (good one for parents who are generally besotted with their children) or their work (some people do very dull jobs, but at least by asking them about it you learn about that area of life). I always ask people:

'What do you do when you are not being dynamic?' followed by: 'Are you a lethal tennis player, a frustrated opera singer, an obsessed fisherman?'

Which leads to mild laughter – and to surprising places. Touch on a person's interests and you will have their attention for ages. I have often managed to go through entire parties without anyone asking me anything about my life.

Who do you know who is generally shunned, politely ignored and avoided by yourself and others? The people who have a very hard life and a terribly lonely time. The people who most need a kind word or act to lift their spirits.

Love thy Neighbour – How to be a Good Samaritan

Most people have heard of the parable of the Good Samaritan. Jesus tells a lawyer that he should 'love thy neighbour as thyself'. 'Who is my neighbour?' replies the man. (Can be quite pedantic, these lawyers.) Jesus then says:

> A man was travelling from Jerusalem to Jericho, and he fell among robbers, who stripped him and beat him, and departed, leaving him half dead. By chance a certain priest was going down that way. When he saw him, he passed by on the other side. In the same way a Levite also, when he came to the place, and saw him, passed by on the other side. But a certain Samaritan, as he travelled, came where he was. When he saw him, he was moved with compassion, came to him, and bound up his wounds, pouring on oil and wine. He set him on his own animal, and brought him to an inn, and took care of him. On the

next day, when he departed, he took out two denarii, and gave them to the host, and said to him, 'Take care of him. Whatever you spend beyond that, I will repay you when I return.'

Now which of these three do you think seemed to be a neighbour to him who fell among the robbers?

He [the lawyer] said, He who showed mercy on him.

Then Jesus said to him, Go and do likewise.

The point of the parable is that both the priest and the Levite, who were extremely important Jewish leaders, left the poor man to die. While the Samaritan, who was not considered of pure blood, and was looked upon as the lowest of the low, stopped and helped. Those who should have and could have helped didn't. The person considered least likely to help did so.

The first question the priest and the Levite asked was: 'If I stop to help this man, what will happen to me?' The Good Samaritan reversed the questions and asked: 'If I do not stop to help this man, what will happen to him?'

Now own up. How many times have you deliberately 'passed by on the other side', ignored someone's plea for help, or knew that someone was having a difficult time but avoided asking them about it and 'getting too close'. You might have hurried on with your own life, because after all you are very busy, and someone else will step in.

Jesus did not spend his time on earth mixing with the great and good, or the powerful and influential. He did exactly the opposite. He went out of his way to help the poor and the weak, to heal the sick, and associated with prostitutes and tax collectors. It is these acts of kindness and healing for which he is remembered.

Small Ways to Help Others

A friend of mine told me this story: 'Once, when our three children were very, very young (three under the age of three), a friend rang in the middle of the afternoon and said, "Don't cook supper. I'm bringing some round at 5 p.m." We waited with great anticipation. Sure enough, on the pip of 5, she appeared with a chicken casserole, new potatoes and salad, and we had supper handed over to us on the doorstep. This gift really touched us and has inspired me to do the same. A cake or supper – unsolicited – makes people's hearts soft. It's simple, unexpected and it works. Surprise is definitely a key element!'

We now have a great neighbourhood Food Chain. People volunteer to cook and deliver meals on an informal rota. When someone's in hospital, has a sick child, a new baby, a bereavement, is convalescing – whatever it is that's making life difficult – the group is alerted, contact made and a meal delivered, sometimes regular meals over several weeks. People with large freezers keep back-up supplies, but most is out-of-the oven fresh. Many of those helped try at first to insist they can cope REALLY, but in truth they are touched by the kindness, the notion that someone they don't even know has taken the time out to do this for them, and cheered by contact with someone who's set aside some time to brighten up their day. The impact is much greater than a good supper.

And you won't be surprised to learn that the people cooking and delivering all this food find the whole experience very rewarding, especially being alerted to people who need some extra TLC at lots of levels besides food – but would never normally broadcast it.

CHARITY BEGINS AT HOME

Here is a starting list of practical things that you could do to help people. I am sure that you can think of many more of your own. Little things matter a lot. It *is* the thought that counts, but the *action* that matters:

1. Visit someone you know who isn't well. Take them a small treat, some flowers, chocolate, fruit, a good magazine, a DVD, a cooked meal, supplies from the local supermarket. Or ring them to find out how they are. Leave enough time for them to tell you.
2. Visit someone you don't know who is in hospital. Ring the local hospital, ask for their visitors' group and ask them who needs cheering up.
3. Offer to take people to and from hospital for their appointments. A friend once volunteered to take a boy who had been hurt playing hockey to hospital. She did so, waited for him to be treated and took him back to the school. She has continued to do school 'medical runs' for several years.
4. Take someone elderly or disabled shopping. Or add their shopping list to yours. Or to an appointment with their doctor or dentist. Or to their local library. Allow extra time for slower progress and nattering!
5. Call a friend and ask them how they are. What news in their world? Easy to do at lunchtime if you are at work, or in the evening or at a weekend. Leave enough time to swap news, talk and listen.
6. Email or text someone, or better still, send them a card. How's the studying / work / fitness programme / diet / love life? I use postcards from art galleries, museums and card shops to send thanks, ideas and thoughts to people. Even if it seems a little old-fashioned it seems

somehow more personal.
7. Send some flowers to a friend (or cut some from your garden).
8. Ask a friend / friends round to share a meal with you. We are not talking dinner parties and hard work. Quick, simple food – pasta, salad and a bottle of wine will be enough. It's their news, gossip and company that you want.
9. Ask someone you don't really know, or wouldn't normally ask, home for supper. Random acts of kindness broaden the mind! (See pages 62–63 – Join Me.)
10. Give a child or some children a treat. Take them to a park with a ball or a kite, a cinema, a circus or pantomime, a football match, or even out for a meal. If the thought appeals but panics you, pair up with a friend to do it.
11. Offer to take young children away from their parents for half a day or a day, to give the parents some downtime. They will love you for it.
12. Offer to babysit for nothing so that parents or a single mum can go out for the evening. Read the child a book, or let them read to you, or just watch television together.
13. Lend or give someone some money, and don't ask for or expect to get it back.
14. Help someone who is fed up with their job to get another job. Give them the names of three people who could help them.
15. Meet a friend for a cappuccino, a drink or lunch. Listen to their world. Don't go into 'transmit' mode. Ask if there is anything you can do to help them. For some extraordinary reason people often only tell you what is

really bothering them during the last five minutes of a conversation.
16. Buy someone a night out to the theatre, or the cinema.
17. Tell someone when they have done something well. Books are written about the importance of this – but the bottom line is that praising people for doing something well has a huge impact on their self-esteem.
18. Thank someone for something that they have done for you.

FIONA'S STORY

Fiona became involved with the Kensington Day Centre after hearing a talk at one of their fundraising events. She was very struck by what a difference fairly low-key interventions, such as assisted bathing and chiropody, made to the mobility and well-being of local elderly people, and how easily the vulnerable elderly could 'fall out of the loop' as a result of illness, decreased mobility or the loss of carer or partner, and how the friendly support of the Centre staff could help them regain their footing again.

Her daughter was moved to organise a fun run at her primary school and during a subsequent visit to the Centre the girls talked with many of the members. They were surprised by how few of the old people were able to visit their favourite local places, such as the newly refurbished cinema or the flowers in the nearby gardens, and they began to ask them what they would most like to do if they had the opportunity. The answers were many and varied: a visit to the pub; fish and chips at the seaside; a cream tea in a beautiful garden. All of these simple pleasures were so achievable that it really motivated the girls not only to want to raise the funds to enable these wishes but to become more involved with the Centre. They are now planning a visit to the cinema for a matinée performance followed by tea, which they hope will be the first of many outings. Fiona tells me how special it was to see how important the realisation of these wishes was to the children and how much pleasure their desire gave these elderly people.

> The Kensington Day Centre
> Convent Gardens
> Kensington Park Road
> London W11 1NJ
> Tel: 0207 727 7337
> → www.octaviahousing.org.uk

WE ARE WHAT WE DO

We Are What We Do is a movement created to inspire people to use their everyday actions to change the world. And that includes you. Since the publication of their first book, *Change the World for a Fiver*, they have made films, given lectures, published German, Australian and Canadian editions, worked with schools and corporate environments, published another book – *Change the World 9 to 5* – and given us the Anya Hindmarch 'I'm Not A Plastic Bag'. Their first nationwide campaign, 'Decline Plastic Bags', aimed to reduce the 10 billion bags a year used by UK consumers. Each of these bags takes 500 years to degrade. Declining plastic bags is now seen as acceptable, responsible and cool, and most of the major supermarkets now have alternatives to and/or incentives not to use them.

In *Change the World for a Fiver* (which has sold an amazing 750,000 copies) the movement created 100 simple, everyday actions that can improve our environment, our health and our communities, and make our planet and the people on it much happier. The website has logged the following actions as the most popular ten:

1. **Smile and smile back.**
2. **Decline plastic bags wherever possible.**
3. **Turn off the tap whilst you brush your teeth.**
4. **Turn off unnecessary lights.**
5. **Fit at least one energy-saving lightbulb.**
6. **Take public transport when you can.**
7. **Hug someone.**
8. **Read a story with a child.**
9. **Use a mug not a plastic cup.**
10. **Try watching less TV.**

→ www.wearewhatwedo.org

Start a Giving Club

No one knows how many book clubs there are; some estimate there could be as many as 50,000. Groups of friends meeting together on a regular basis to read and discuss books on any variety of topics, from the latest novel to biographies and gardening books.

One of my ambitions is to get *The More You Give, The More You Get* chosen by as many book clubs as possible, for two rather obvious reasons. Firstly, of course, it would help sales of the book! Secondly, on a more philanthropic level, it would encourage groups of people meeting all over the UK to discuss the whole issue of giving.

This might lead to the formation of new Giving Clubs, groups of people who discuss the needs in their local community, or a national or international issue, and then take action to help. In Chapter 3 you can read about The Funding Network, a rather advanced and practical model of this idea. (See pages 82–84.)

JOIN ME

Danny Wallace was described, in the *Financial Times* no less, as 'the nicest kind of idiot'. Some idiot. Danny is a comedian, writer, presenter of the BBC2 programme *Castaway*, and the founder of 'a cult' called Join Me (as well as starting his own country – but that's another story, DVD etc). The cult's aims are to encourage its members to carry out Random Acts of Kindness for a complete stranger every Friday, subsequently named Good Fridays. Through his websites, and his book – *Random Acts of Kindness: 365 Ways to Make the World a Nicer Place* – he has built up a semi-worldwide movement, the Karma Army, thousands of 'proud and noble followers' who have all signed the 'Good Friday Agreement' and agreed to follow the cult's aim: improving the life of a total stranger, if only for a moment or two, every Friday. Leaving aside the eccentric behaviour, and the obvious good that everyone does, our hero has received messages of support

CHARITY BEGINS AT HOME

from Tony Blair and Prince Charles, and been invited to launch the International Philanthropy workshop.

10 Random Acts of Kindness (selected at random!)

1. Pay for a stranger's meal.
2. Today, give blood. Seriously. Do it. www.blood.co.uk
3. Be unfailingly polite to every single person you meet.
4. Top up a parking meter that's about to run out.
5. Let someone keep the change.
6. Make someone their own personal compilation CD.
7. Hide a book token in a random book in a bookshop.
8. Help a fly or a daddy-long-legs out of your house rather than squashing it.
9. Get an organ donor card.
10. Give a flower seller a fiver and tell them to hand the next person who passes some flowers.

→ www.join-me.co.uk   → www.dannywallace.com

HOWARD'S STORY

One week after the Asian tsunami, Howard Carter arrived at our church in a suit and a tie, itself fairly unusual behaviour. During the service he spoke, and the essence of his story was very inspirational and to the point.

The previous Christmas he had spent with his children at an orphanage in Southern India in which 1,200 children lived. The orphanage itself had survived the horrors of the tsunami, but many of the local villagers – fishermen – had been out at sea in little canoes when the earthquake happened and were missing presumed dead. Around 10,000 refugees, mainly women and children, turned up at the orphanage, depleting all their resources.

Howard's plan was to take a flight to Southern India that afternoon, at his own cost. He was going to take all the water purification kits he could buy and as much money as he could raise to buy food and supplies for the orphanage.

On his arrival in India, everyone was obviously very despondent. Howard brought with him a restorative humour, re-energising the staff and volunteers, and giving much-needed support.

Several weeks later he returned to the church and spoke again, thanking the congregation for their contributions and telling several wonderful, heart-rending stories of kindness, love and practical help.

Howard visited India again the following Christmas having helped organise a training conference which raised over $70,000. A great community hall was built above the Arabian Sea as a shelter, and now doubles as a conference centre.

The following year I went to India and met Frederick, the founder and director of the orphanage. Here was another inspirational doer. After the tsunami the orphanage had swelled by a further 200 children, and his thoughts focused on fishing and the long-term future of children in the fishing villages along that stretch of coast.

Frederick's dream is that none of the 5,000 children under the age of five will grow up to be fishermen, scratching a living at best, risking their lives at worst. 'There is no fish and no future,' he told me. 'The commercial boats 3 miles out take all the fish. The people are starving, even before the tsunami.' Frederick got in touch with the head men in the villages along the coast with a simple proposition: if families with a child under five could commit to save 100 rupees (£1.20) a month for six years, and so deposit 6,000 rupees in a saving fund, he would add a further 20,000 rupees to their saving pot and it would be invested for them until they were eighteen. The families' contribution was essential to get their commitment and involvement and keep their self-respect. It was also manageable. The only thing asked from them is that the children complete their formal schooling. Interest rates in India are historically high and Frederick estimates each individual fund could become worth 80,000 rupees (£1,000). Enough to get out of the poverty trap, go to college, buy a house, or pay for a dowry. And give up fishing. A long-term solution that will help about 5,000 children move out of poverty as they grow up ... and imagine the knock-on impact that could have on the fishing communities they come from, where it's now not uncommon for the catch to be so meagre as to generate less than £5 a month.

Howard's gut response to a disaster and Frederick's vision and huge commitment has led to a potentially huge impact on the lives of thousands of children, their families and the villages they live in.

Two men with a heart for a local community and, importantly, the will to act.

→ www.bethsaidahermitage.com

PATRICK'S HOSPITAL

Patrick Foster spent most of the holiday period between Christmas and New Year 2004 at his desk in the City, watching with increasing horror as the tsunami devastation unfolded. He decided that he wanted to do something to help directly, rather than through any of the established agencies, 'to get his hands dirty', so he set out to raise the money to buy a field hospital. Knowing little about fundraising, and even less about buying a field hospital, he asked the company he worked for, and a small circle of business colleagues and friends, for the funding.

Within two days he found a supplier of field hospitals in America, but needed to find an agency able to staff it. One of his contacts put him in touch with Great Ormond Street hospital, which knew that a field hospital would be desperately needed in Galle, Sri Lanka. Many emails, faxes and phone calls later, he had raised more than $850,000 from the City and major donors, ordered a fifty-bed field hospital from America, completed the due diligence on the supplier – which included speaking to the US special forces – arranged documentation, the commercial contract and the transport for the hospital, and organised the Sri Lankan delivery, location and building of a concrete base and staff.

The hospital in Galle was operational seven weeks after Patrick's idea was born, acting as a day clinic for over fifty people per day as well as a teaching unit for medical students who are the future for Sri Lanka.

Nearly three years later in 2007, Medical Aid to Galle – MAGE (Patrick's original vision has become a registered charity) – has a two-pronged programme for continuing support for the tsunami-affected region of the south-west part of the island.

The next most pressing need was for a hostel for their medical students. The previous hostel was washed out by the tsunami and the students were living in disgusting conditions. Plans were drawn up by local architects and the money was raised to build and equip the hostel: $650,000. The ceremonial foundation stone was laid in December 2006.

Other small, discrete projects have been expanded and include: the support for a disabled children's centre; a young persons' school; and an after school training centre where MAGE pays all the running costs and administrative expenses, plus scholarships for more than a hundred students who lost parents in the tsunami. The scholarships are for medical students who come from the Galle region and have little or no family support, and cover their university fees and living expenses until the end of their courses.

The disabled children's centre is one of the few in the country which offers support, counselling and rehabilitation for families that come from all over the island. When Patrick visited the centre in 2006 a family had just arrived having travelled two days by bus to have their child assessed. MAGE has built a wall around the centre and paid for a full-time guard/janitor to provide security for the staff and patients. They have committed to fund the centre for the next three years.

The trustees have committed to continuing their work and are presently looking at raising money to build a nurses' home.

The man who started all this as a one-off project is now committed for the foreseeable future. He has visited Galle and seen first-hand the impact that his original act of 'active generosity' has had in the local community, and the impact on him has been profound. As he says, 'It is a good question as to who has benefited most.'

→ www.mageuk.org

Chapter 3

HOW TO GIVE TO CHARITY

'You must be the change you wish to see in the world.'
Mahatma Gandhi

You now need to begin to think about the causes and charities that you are really interested in or concerned about, charities you think are doing great work. Then re-focus your efforts on supporting them. Stop being hunted – go hunting!

There are two main things you can give to charity: your money or your time.

Let's go through this in a logical manner. For volunteering see page 85. But let's take money first:

1. How Much Are You Giving at the Moment?

You might find it instructive to work out how much money you have given to various causes in the last year, from sponsoring Jesame's swimming gala at school, to Alistair's London Marathon triumph – lucky you if you only had to sponsor one runner! – or the table at the charity ball that you really didn't want to go to. The result could surprise or shame you.

2. How Much Do You Think You Could Give?

Or to put it another way, now that you are on the way to becoming an enlightened mini-philanthropist, have had a discussion with yourself and or your family about 'what is enough' (see page 28), how much is left over?

3. Which Causes Are You Going to Support?

Think about the causes you care about, genuinely upset you or even make you very angry. (Anger is a surprisingly strong motivator.) It may be a medical condition or disability that has affected a member of your family or a close friend. It could be a social injustice such as homelessness or human rights. It might be a particular arts organisation, theatre, art gallery or opera company that inspires you. You might be getting increasingly concerned about the environment. (You should be!) Or want to support education or disadvantaged youth. Some people prefer their charitable contribution to be spent in their country, town or even street. Others want to help relieve poverty in the developing world where a little money really does go much further, or give something back to the country of their roots. Try not to choose more than three or four causes.

MAIN CHARITY AREAS

- **Culture and the Arts.** All arts organisations need funds and sponsorship to survive and to reach out to disadvantaged and disabled adults and children and arts-starved communities.

- **Sport.** London Olympics in 2012 is imminent, and there are numerous opportunities to fund sports, and young sportsmen and women. Sport keeps disadvantaged young people off the streets and out of trouble, and has a very positive impact on self-esteem and life chances.

- **Homelessness.** This is a complex social issue with numbers of rough sleepers today equalling the situation at the beginning of the last century. There are a wide variety of very good charities, some local, some national, with the emphasis on moving people through to independent living.

- **Education.** A popular area of charitable investment for companies and donors – providing many young people with opportunities to gain a better chance early, as well as broadening their horizons. This area includes charities that work to motivate or engage young people, or campaign for anti-bullying, drugs awareness, literacy, IT, life skills, mentoring, conservation and environment issues.

- **Children and young people.** The care of and for children from unstable and abusive backgrounds. Helping disadvantaged and 'difficult' young people 'outside the system', 'the unloved and unloveable'.

- **Medical.** Drugs and alcohol charities are not 'popular', but do invaluable work.

    Cancer charities are a world of their own – there are nearly 800 of them, ranging from well-known research and care organisations to those dealing with specific cancers. According to some figures, one in three adults will suffer from the disease. Then there are the medical charities that support people with specific conditions such as multiple sclerosis, heart disease, Parkinson's and diabetes.

• **Disability.** At least 10 million people in the UK have some form of disability. Only 15 per cent are born with their disability; most become disabled through accident or health problems they suffer after birth. There are a huge variety of charities supporting, for example, visual impairment, deafness, learning difficulties, mental health, loss of limbs, spinal injury, equipment support, IT access and life-long care.

• **Overseas aid.** Even allowing for the problems of monitoring distribution, which is carried out effectively by some larger charities who understand the local politics and very small charities who avoid intermediaries, £1 does go much further in Africa, India etc than in the UK. It is possible to build a school for under £10,000 and provide fresh drinking water for an entire village for £1,000. And yes, there is corruption, so you do have to be careful.

• **The environment.** If you really don't think there isn't a problem with global warming, climate change, desertification and population growth, first of all give yourself a sharp slap, then buy a copy of Al Gore's DVD *The Inconvenient Truth*, then go on to the Friends of the Earth website (www.foe.co.uk), then take action, then apologise to your friends and family. Especially your children. (See also page 111.)

- **Other important areas.** These include: social care (carer organisations, counselling, respite care for a variety of needs, community centres, volunteer projects, family support work, domestic abuse); conservation, animals and wildlife; human rights; welfare of the elderly; hospices; other social needs catered for by the Samaritans and others.

4. Which Charities?

Research the charities working in your areas of interest. Maybe friends are already involved with a particular charity. Ask them about the cause, their support and the work they do. Go onto a charity's website, download or send off for their annual report and other information, although try not to become a financial analyst at this stage: you are searching for the compassionate you, not the accountant. Try Guidestar (www.guidestar.org.uk.), a comprehensive source of information of charity activities and finances available free to the public, or better still, download the excellent reports on areas of charity work and individual charities from New Philanthropy Capital (www.philanthropycapital.org, see pages 191–192). The Intelligent Giving website is also terrific (see below). Identify the organisations operating in your areas of interest. Where are they based? What do they do? Do they have any projects that need funding now and in the future? Could they use your particular talents and skills?

INTELLIGENT GIVING

Intelligent Giving is a small, not-for-profit, independent company based in Bethnal Green, London, and is for everyone interested in giving to charities. To their eternal credit they sometimes upset people in the charity world, most famously this year having 'a spat' with Children in Need about their transparency and the way they present their 'costs' to the public.

Their excellent free public website, with a welcome sense of mischief and humour, has a searchable database of more than 1,300 charities which would interest donors. They are intuitively categorised – easy to find and compare – and the top 500 have been profiled and ranked by transparency, with at-a-glance icons showing reserves, highest salary, overall expenditure and more. There are sections on how to give your money and your time – it lists every volunteering website in the UK – plus expert opinions, interviews with givers and doers, and the truth about certain rumours: fat cat bosses, Princess Diana, the Donkey Sanctuary, public schools, and many more. It's entertaining, easy to use, informative and fun. One for your web 'favourites'.

→ www.intelligentgiving.com

5. Consider Supporting a Small, or Medium-size Charity

In today's world, small and medium-size charities are more vulnerable than the larger organisations. They have less resources and reserves against a rainy day, and do not have the enormous mailing lists, fundraising departments and donor bases that the larger charities have built up over time. They may need your help more urgently.

6. Plan Your Giving

You have decided on the causes that interest you. Now organise your donation. Your first mission is to work out how much you can afford to give, and, most importantly, to give it tax-effectively (see next page). What we are talking about is consolidating your financial giving into an organised programme. Regular donations are hugely important because they enable charities to plan, and to survive a setback to the economy, or the rain bucketing down on the day of the outdoor fundraising event.

Planning your giving in an effective way is hugely rewarding. Focusing your financial firepower, and your other talents, in one or two areas can have remarkable results. You become proactive, seeking out the causes and charities that interest you and making a difference. You are no longer reactive, responding to the best-written letter, the most heart-rending appeal, or a request from a business colleague to support their cause, writing out cheques to anyone who asks and 'binning' all charitable requests. This is a much more exciting and liberating position to be in.

7. How Are You Going to Give Your Funds?

A one-off donation using gift aid? Through payroll giving, gifts of shares, reviewing your will to leave money to your chosen causes? This might also be a good time to consider setting aside a portion of your weekly, monthly, annual income to give away, so-called 'tithing' (see page 77). Whether it's 2 per cent or 10 per cent, you will almost certainly not miss it. Rather like a direct debit you take out, once done it will really not be noticed and life will go on. Even when you do experience tough financial times you are less likely to cut back on the relatively small amount that you give to a cause, because it represents the better you.

CHARITIES AID FOUNDATION

A CAF charity account provides you with a dedicated bank account to manage your charity donations, allowing you to give however much you wish, whenever you like. You get your own cheque book and CAF reclaims the tax. (Please read the section below on tax-effective giving!) You can even make your donations anonymously. They can also help you start a private foundation (see page 184), shape its mission and advise you on grant-making to give your philanthropy real focus. They can also handle the legal and administrative side. CAF also manages Give As You Earn, the largest payroll-giving scheme in the UK.

You can apply online at www.cafonline.org or telephone 01732 520 050.

---

8. Tax-Effective Giving

Please don't glaze over! The financial benefits of being

organised are substantial. Under the Gift Aid scheme, for every £1 that is donated, charities can claim an extra 28p from HM Revenue & Customs. So if you give £100, the charity will receive £128, the extra being contributed by the taxman at no extra cost to the donor. All you have to do is provide your address and tax status. And if you are a 40 per cent taxpayer, you can claim back another 18 per cent either for yourself, or to pass on to the charity. It makes a big difference to the charity.

£1,000 given sensibly to charity each year becomes £1,280 (at 28 per cent) or £1,510 (at 40 per cent); while £10,000 becomes £12,800 (at 28 per cent) or £15,100 (at 40 per cent).

Incredibly, two-thirds of charitable giving in Britain is made without using this scheme. Charities Aid Foundation estimates this amount as a staggering £1 billion, literally being thrown away.

A few companies operate payroll-giving schemes that automatically deduct the amount you choose to give to charity from your payslip. Painless! Ask if your employer has such an arrangement. Donations made this way are deducted before tax, giving immediate tax relief. This means that a gift of £10 costs a basic rate taxpayer £7.80, and a higher rate taxpayer £6. The best companies match their employees' contribution. For example RBS, one of the most generous supporters of payroll giving, gives £2 for every £1 given by their employees.

For higher tax rate donors the situation can become more complex. Payment of any bonus direct from the company, rather than from the individual, to the charity is worth serious consideration.

Large, one-off donations can only be offset against

income tax or capital gains tax actually paid in a year, although this can be backdated one year provided that you have not submitted your tax return for the previous tax year. Alternatively, the total sum may be donated over a period of years to achieve maximum impact for the charity.

Tax relief is also available for gifts of shares to charity, which would relieve the donor of any capital gains tax charge and (in the case of quoted securities) give him an income tax deduction as well! When it comes to shares, all the tax relief goes to the donor – the charity does not recover any tax. If you want to give shares it is worth contacting Sharegift (www.sharegift.org.uk) who can take the paperwork off your hands.

The relief on giving shares has now been extended to the gifting of land to charity, but the rules are complex and you must take proper advice.

(Note: with effect from 1 April 2008, basic rate tax becomes 25 per cent, so some of the above figures will change!)

TITHING

Tithing was common in many ancient societies and cultures throughout the Middle East in pre-biblical times. It is mentioned several times in the Bible and played a key part of Jewish law and religion in those days. In Europe, tithing became an important means of supporting the established churches, their buildings, their clergy and the poor in each community, probably in that order. The more of a legal duty it became, the less popular the system was.

When I first heard about tithing I felt it was out of order. Didn't people know that I had commitments, a mortgage, credit card debts, holidays to pay for, children's clothes to buy, school fees to survive, pension contributions to make for my old age? I thought indignantly. Look, when I am financially stable, then I will gladly give money away to others. Till then, *please* leave me alone.

Then one day I met a young man who earned very little and yet still gave away 10 per cent of his income. I thought, if he can do it, there is very little excuse for me not to, so I started very modestly, giving just a little of my monthly income. Shortly afterwards I received a pay rise, and really, in a sense of gratitude, it seemed quite reasonable to give a small percentage of that away as well. I began gradually to increase my monthly giving until it reached 10 per cent of my earnings.

This personal and financial commitment is important. It will make you feel much better about yourself, especially in your 'down days' when you are in 'full moan mode'. When a portion of your income and wealth is set aside for helping others you won't take yourself so seriously. Putting something back into life that creates value for others and yourself also helps you to be thankful for what you've got, as well as recognising that you can quite adequately live off less. Being able to mentally draw the line at what is 'enough' – as in the Tolstoy story on page 26 – is a big step in growing up, a paradigm shift.

However, some people argue that the principle of tithing is flawed. A person earning £100,000 who gives away or tithes 10 per cent of his income is giving £10,000 but still has £90,000 left, which is still a great deal of money to live off, save, invest, or spend otherwise. A person earning £10,000 a year and tithing 10 per cent is left with £9,000, which could and probably will make his life harder. And once someone has mentally grasped the value of tithing 10 per cent of their income, there is a strong chance that they will hit a mental 'giving ceiling', sit back and feel pleased with themselves that they have done their bit. But those on high incomes can easily manage 10 per cent *and* be free to give more when need be.

If you decide to tithe, should the amount be from your gross income or your net income? This has been debated for years, but I'm afraid I rather take the view that I give away a percentage of what I actually receive, i.e. my net income. Maybe I will go gross as I mature!

9. Discretionary Pot

When you have planned the majority of your giving, put aside 10 per cent of it for discretionary giving: to support a child who is doing a sponsored spell at school; to give a work colleague who is collecting for the local hospice that treated their wife or husband; to go to a friend's charity dinner (they will have to come to yours!); or to contribute to Children in Need, Comic Relief or a shocking international disaster like Darfur. In other words, don't go into hiding, just become organised.

10. Put Your Chosen Charities in Your Will

What do you mean, you haven't got a will? This is the holy grail of fundraising. Legacy income is the largest source of voluntary income to charities – one-third of the total income of Cancer Research UK and 50 per cent of the income of the RSPCA, for example – and is worth a whopping £1.3 billion each year, though still only 4.3 per cent of us include a charity in our will.

And it is hugely cost-effective. Someone pops off to the next world and on the way out sends the charity a cheque, which is paid before tax is deducted from their estate, thereby cutting the amount of inheritance tax due.

A word of warning. This may be against the spirit of the book but charities would love you to leave them your *residuary estate*. That is the amount left over after you have sorted out what you wish to leave to your nearest and dearest. They know that your assets are likely to increase significantly after you have made your will, and that, with a bit of luck, the residuary estate could be the most valuable part of it. If you're happy with that, fine; if not, leave a set amount, or a percentage, to the charities of your choice.

OTHER WAYS TO SUPPORT A CHARITY

- Fundraise. Organise an event and send the charity the net profit.
- Run a marathon. Yes, you can! I did and look what happened to me. Plus you will become seriously fit and feel great.
- Offer to speak about the charity, or collect a cheque

at an event or school assembly. It will save the organisation the cost of having to send someone from their office.
- Become a trustee of a charity or a governor at a local school. Save them the effort and resources spent looking for you. Look for them.
- Volunteer (see below).
- Supply gifts in kind; if you are a printer, offer to print material at cost.
- If your firm is moving premises and getting new office furniture and IT equipment for a brave new world, offer the old desks and computers to a charity – but only if they work.
- Offer management or skills support. Are you a marketing brain, an IT guru or an accountant?
- Recycle print cartridges, phones and paper.
- Take clothes (clean!), toys, books and unwanted Christmas presents to charity shops.

11. Involving Others

This is a good time to start gathering a small group of people who you think might be interested in helping you support your new venture. From those who may already support the cause to those you think might be interested and helpful. There's much more power, and enjoyment, in a group. Think of everyone you know – family, friends, colleagues at your company or school. You are likely to come across several like minded people, and if you don't you can use your new enthusiasm and enormous powers of persuasion to sell them your cause.

THE FUNDING NETWORK

The Funding Network (TFN) is an open-to-all organisation that brings donors together and runs funding 'events', where charities present their cases for funding and donors give as a group. As they say: 'We work together, eat together, dance together, yet mostly give alone. Giving is more enjoyable and more powerful when done by a group, and what you can give certainly seems to go further.'

Over the course of a day, including a break for a sociable lunch, up to ten organisations are given a twelve-minute slot to present to the hundred or so attendees – the first six minutes to explain their cause, the next six to answer questions. Time-keeping is strict. At the end of the day the audience is invited to make donations, which are written up on a flipchart as they are shouted out. There is no obligation to give at all, but people do get inspired by hearing the projects, and there is always a buzz at the pledging session. Though the most common gift is £100 to an individual project, participants will often give several thousand pounds. The Funding Network bundles all the gifts to each project together, reclaims Gift Aid where appropriate, and sends a single cheque. The grant to any given project depends of course on what people have pledged, but is generally around £7,000, and the total for a day is usually £50,000 to £70,000.

As one attendee said, the most exciting part of the day is hearing the stories: 'Only one of them was for me a bit dull. The others were one or more of the following:

gripping, inspiring, eye-opening, moving, funny, impressive, challenging, dramatic . . . All of them made me feel glad to be learning something I didn't know. Most of all it was a privilege listening to them, and the last part calling out the donations was exciting, too.'

I so enjoyed going to The Funding Network that I became a member. It *is* fun giving as a group, and I always discover interesting, small charities doing remarkable work that I have never heard of. The variety of causes is fascinating and inspiring and different.

Only members of The Funding Network can propose charities, by sponsoring them and putting up the first 'donation' or bid themselves. Typically, in the course of a year, 100 organisations are put forward and thirty chosen to make a presentation. The Network favours smaller charities and new ventures, taking risks which other funders might turn away from.

Here are some examples from one day's presentations:

Fight for Peace started in the favelas of Rio de Janiero where children and adolescents are employed by drug factions as openly armed foot soldiers, lookouts and drug sellers. The charity teaches the disciplines of boxing. At their annual 'sports day' over two thousand young people turn up to watch, guns and knives are banned, and even gang leaders cross boundaries and obey the rules. Funding was needed to open a UK branch in Tower Hamlets. (Email: luke@vivario.org.br)

ITEZO in Zambia gives formal education and skills training to sustain widows and orphans affected by the AIDS pandemic.

RENUE teaches pupils in Southwark schools about

renewable energy.

Sing London aims to encourage everyone in the capital to sing (research showing it's great for health and happiness). All kinds of people singing all kinds of music in all kinds of places. (www.singlondon.org)

The Helen Bamber Foundation is a UK-based human rights organisation dedicated to providing help, care and treatment for women who have suffered human rights violations and have been traumatised by their experiences. (www.helenbamber.org)

Green Knickers was created by two enthusiastic young women who had designed and made fun and sexy Fair Trade organic underwear. (www.greenknickers.org)

The Corporate Watch Service is a research group supporting campaigns which are increasingly successful in forcing corporations to behave in a better way. (www.corporatewatch.org.uk)

Fallujah was a piece of documentary theatre (every word direct reportage) about the siege of this Iraqi town, acknowledging the injustices as it was flattened by the Americans during the Iraq War.

Ms Mpatheleni Makaulule built the Luvhola Cultural Village in South Africa to protect the communal land and sacred sites of the culture and traditions of her people, the Venda. She now wishes to assist three communities to secure legal rights to protect and manage key sacred and ecologically sensitive sites in their area, which are being destroyed by inappropriate industrial development.

For more information or to join, phone 0207 243 0667 or log on to www.thefundingnetwork.org.uk

Volunteering

There is something slightly dull about the word 'volunteering'. It conjures up thoughts of worthiness, doing something dull for free, which we haven't got time for, and of suspect government initiatives. It's just not an exciting word or an inspirational one. Boring.

So I'm challenging you to think: fun, meeting new people, learning new skills, using ones you have, even changing your view of life as you know it. Your community needs you. Projects round the world need you. Time to start exploring!

Not enough money comes through taxes and donations to pay for all the work that needs to be done in the world. Yes, governments should do it all, but they won't. There are too many competing calls on their money, resources and often even their will. They reflect our priorities – and our selfishness. Helping those more in need than ourselves is way down the vote-wining list. So, in a very real sense, volunteering is a very personal statement: a way we can do our bit to make the world a better place.

> *Without the work hours of volunteers, countless wounds will not be tended, mouths will not be fed, grieving people will not be comforted, broken marriages will not be mended, lonely people will not be embraced, children will not be nurtured.* Bill Hybels, The Volunteer Revolution: Unleashing the Power of Everybody

Most of us claim to work hard, but how many of us have a real sense of meaning and purpose in our lives? We have highs at work but also deadlines and stress. Our work may fund our living expenses, our homes, holidays, children, their education, our cars, even our pensions, but there is normally not much left, if anything. And we often don't feel full of life, laughter and bounce in the evenings. We get home late, knackered and stressed, and reach for a drink. Most of us work to live.

Start doing something for others – something which you've chosen to do for no reward – and you will feel valued and worthwhile, energised in a new way. Writing out a cheque to a charity is less demanding but nothing like as rewarding. You will learn new skills, develop talents and gifts you didn't know you had, and can use your passion, ideas, enthusiasm, compassion, love, money and time.

When you become a volunteer you enter another world, meet different people, and become part of a team who look at your contribution, good humour and readiness to muck in, rather than label you by your job.

You really can change the world, and the life of another person – albeit in a small way. It is hugely worth it.

A stranger is walking on a beach when he notices a young man picking up starfish and throwing them back into the sea.

He asks the young man what he is doing. He replies that he is throwing the starfish back in the sea so that they will live. The stranger points out that there are thousands of starfish on the beach, and on all the other beaches along the coast and says: 'But you can't possibly make a difference.'

The young man smiles, throws another starfish

> back and replies, 'Made a difference to that one.'
> As the Talmud says: 'To save one life is as if you have saved the world.'

Your choice is a simple one. You can either carry on thinking about being useful, put it off till a better time and leave it to other people, or you can roll up your sleeves and change your corner of the world.

You will not be alone. About half the adult population in Britain volunteer. Approximately 22 million people. The most popular areas to be involved in are sport and exercise – with ever more opportunities in the lead-up to the 2012 Olympics – children's education and schools, religion and health and social welfare. At least 66 per cent help with fundraising, 55 per cent with an event or activity, and 36 per cent contribute by becoming a committee member.

Volunteering is acknowledged as a hugely positive way to develop young people, and with this comes government funding to encourage volunteering and especially youth volunteering. Part of me rails at the bureaucracy and cost of it all – do we really need the language of infrastructure agencies, quality standards and awards for volunteering? – but young people being useful creates a sense of belonging and respect and reduces anti-social behaviour. It may even create the next generation of great citizens and philanthropists.

Websites now exist to link all ages and skills to all sorts of projects. They have their limitations, but here are some of the best known. It's worth remembering that the lonely pensioner or neighbour who has had a stroke will never hit these databases, so it's worth finding out what's happening on your doorstep as well. Helping very locally will build your sense of community and can be just as rewarding.

VOLUNTEERING WEBSITES

www.csv.org.uk
the UK's largest volunteering and training organisation
www.do-it.org.uk
national online database of opportunities, with a focus on youth
www.g-nation.co.uk
part of the Citizenship Foundation, focus on schools
www.intelligentgiving.com
go to 'give your time' for links to a whole variety of global and local volunteering opportunities
www.pilotlight.org.uk
linking 'proven leaders and high fliers' to small, innovative charities
www.reach-online.org.uk
matching skilled professionals as volunteers
www.timebank.org.uk
inspiring a new generation of people to volunteer in the UK
www.volunteering.org.uk
developing quality volunteering in England
www.vso.org.uk
skilled professionals supporting developing countries
www.wearev.com
championing youth volunteering in England

Volunteering at Work

Does your employer co-ordinate an employee volunteer scheme? You might be able to link up and support their chosen charity or community programme (three-quarters of FTSE 100 companies have some kind of employee volunteer scheme).

Getting Started

Most of the volunteering websites have online application forms which ask the obvious questions, but let's flesh it out a little.

Firstly, think of the time you could give. It could be as little as an hour a week, a day a month, a half-day over the weekend, or more. Be realistic as well as enthusiastic. Under-commit rather than over-commit at first. Better to dip your toe in the water and see whether you are enthused by the work and the organisation, than jump into a new world and be disappointed. Experiment; you might not find the right opportunity immediately, even if you find the right cause.

Now identify your skills and talents, both professional and personal. It is easiest to match your skill set with doing something useful, but quite often using another buried talent is more inspirational and rewarding.

Give some thought to the best way in which *you* feel that you can help a charity. Everyday voluntary tasks are important, and are often straightforward and enjoyable. They need to be done, require time and commitment, but they usually don't need much brainpower.

A great many very busy and successful people don't have

much spare time, but this doesn't mean that they cannot or will not want to contribute. High-flying managers can find an hour spent reading with a child a break that's as good as a rest. Often they are never asked because people assume they are too busy. This is a big mistake. Research shows that the overwhelming reason people volunteer to do something is – wait for it – because they were asked!

You may be invited to do something very simple, way below your actual capacity, and boring beyond belief. There are important jobs to do in all organisations that are demanding and need the use of a good brain, experience or expertise, and it may be a question of getting to know the charity, spotting the need and promoting yourself as the solution. A few hours input from someone experienced in accounting, web design or management performance can make an enormous, long-term impact.

> *Never doubt that a small group of thoughtful, committed citizens can change the world. Indeed, it is the only thing that ever has.* Margaret Mead, anthropologist

Now call up the organisation/s you've selected, ask them if they need help – they invariably will – what opportunities they have and if they could use the sort of skills you think you have. You will learn a lot by the different responses you get, the level of enthusiasm coming down the other end of the phone, and the efficiency with which your questions are answered. If they don't know, or faff about, move on.

A word of warning: you are asking them what help they need to do their work. You may want to spend time caring for disabled, disadvantaged children – being a modern-day Father Christmas – but you will usually need training, to say nothing of a police check before you can be let loose on any vulnerable group. Today's risk assessment culture, with its climate of targets and outputs means any charity taking you on as a volunteer is making quite an investment in you.

Go and meet the organisation. Get a good picture of what the work involves and how the management operates. Ask them if they have got something useful for you to do, and why they want you to do it. What sort of training and support is given to volunteers? Is there a job description? Do they cover expenses such as fares and petrol? It is important to get this information at the start. Think of it as a partnership, marrying your skills, time and enthusiasm to their in-depth knowledge of the area concerned and their organisational ability.

Incidentally, the worst thing that can happen to a volunteer is that you become enthused, set aside time, tell your friends about your new interest, and then turn up to find nothing to do that day, or to be asked by the volunteer leader to do something deathly dull without an obvious purpose. And from their perspective, you saying you will do something and not pitching up is equally annoying.

Entrepreneurial Volunteering

You do not need to work for a charity. You can create an 'entrepreneurial' initiative yourself. Bill Hybels turned the volunteer process on its head by encouraging people to create their own exciting new initiatives. If you have a particular talent he encourages you to use it, admittedly for a higher purpose, but immediately for practical use. In *The Volunteer Revolution* he gives some great examples of how numerous new volunteer ideas were born in his community.

A hairdresser got some friends together and offered free hairdressing to residents at the local nursing home and a centre for disabled people. A group then started teaching hairdressing skills to women and young girls working as prostitutes, providing them with new means to earn a living.

Another group started a food brokerage, collecting food from the local community, sorting and distributing it to hungry families for whom buying food of any sort was an expense, and a challenge.

One woman started a family fostering programme; another a refugee welcoming programme, which helped families to set up their first home, settle into the community, sign on with a doctor, a school, taking with them clothes and food and whatever else was needed.

Expert water-skiers took young people away for the weekend and taught them how to water-ski.

One my favourites is CARS, which stands for Christian Auto Repairmen Servicing (only in America!). Cars are donated to CARS by people in the church and community, repaired and given to others who have fallen on hard times, quite often single mums. And they then continue to service the cars for free. They're not qualified mechanics, just people really interested in tinkering with cars – whom Bill endearingly calls 'Gearheads'. (There's a similar scheme in the UK. See www.timebank.org.uk.)

The message is that we all have talents and skills that we can use to help out in the world, that volunteering can be

HOW TO GIVE TO CHARITY

original, fun and a huge blessing to the givers as well as the receivers. Ask yourself: what could I do, and what would I like to do? Why on earth wouldn't I want to be involved in something useful and fun?

Just get on with it. Becoming a volunteer can have a profound and very positive impact on your own life, and the lives of others.

There is a wonderful sign on the wall of Shishu Bhavan, a children's home in Calcutta, called 'Anyway'. It reads:

People are unreasonable, illogical and self-centred.
Love them anyway.
If you do good, people will accuse you of selfish, ulterior motives.
Do good anyway.
If you are successful, you will win false friends and true enemies.
Succeed anyway.
The good you do today will be forgotten tomorrow.
Do good anyway.
Honesty and frankness will make you vulnerable.
Be honest and frank anyway.
What you spent years building may be destroyed overnight.
Build anyway.
People really need help but may attack you if you help them.
Help people anyway.
Give the world the best you have and you'll get kicked in the teeth.
Give the world the best you've got anyway.

And Finally . . .

Putting Money into Collection Boxes

At least 18 per cent of the public give to charities in this 'ad hoc' way. I always feel that if people are prepared to give up their morning and freeze to death outside a railway station or a local supermarket to collect money for their chosen cause, it is mean not to give them couple of quid. And don't get prissy and refuse their daffodil sticker or whatever; take it and wear it with pride – at the very least it will stop other collectors approaching you.

The *Big Issue*

A great initiative to help homeless people out of their Catch 22 (you can't get a place to live without a job, or a job without a permanent address). It has grown and grown. Treat as above. I find many of the sellers very cheery and anyone who is into making an effort gets my vote. Same goes for people busking in the street, in the Underground and so on. They are making a contribution and sometimes making life 'smilier'. But I do have a problem with being trapped in a train as someone takes up their guitar to serenade me!

Beggars

Tricky one, this. The serious arguments are that giving beggars money creates a viable street economy and keeps them out of service-providing organisations that can genuinely help them. Thames Reach (www.thamesreach.org.uk), a highly-regarded charity working with homeless people, has been running a campaign called 'Killing with Kindness'. In their view 'contrary to popular perception, most people who beg are not homeless'. Westminster Council in London agrees. Their survey showed that 86 per cent of people begging spend the cash they receive on drugs and alcohol. Seven out of ten beggars arrested in Westminster in 2005 tested positive for Class A drugs. Thames Reach says: 'In the experience of frontline workers, people are more likely to accept help and to address their addictions when they are not receiving money from begging.'

That said, some of the waffle about them 'all living in good houses in the suburbs and driving Ferraris' has always struck me as far-fetched. Many are genuinely marginalised, invisible people on the fringes of society, some of whom have mental health problems, have run away from an unhappy home, have suffered abuse and/or have a serious addiction problem.

In an ideal world you should give them money through a proper agency. If you have given money to people who 'only need £1.40p to get back to Newcastle' more than once, shake yourself hard.

The National Lottery

What to make of the National Lottery? Set up to provide a proportion of its profits to good causes and 'robbed' on a regular basis to pay for enterprises like the Olympics, and for what used to be called government expenditure. And, on a bad day, given to presenting very large sums of money to very strange causes. But still a source of badly needed funds to a very broad range of organisations struggling to improve their part of the world.

Of course there is a feeling that, for some people, playing the lottery is a substitute for giving to charity. Those against it cite this argument, and the fact that it is a tax on the innumerate, as anyone really believing that a 1 in 13,983,816 chance of matching all six numbers and winning is a good deal will almost certainly lose their money.

Chapter 4

CHARITY WORLD

'Some people say that if we give charity to others it'll diminish the responsibility of government towards the needy and the poor. I don't concern myself with this because governments don't usually offer love. I just do what I can do: the rest is not my business.'

Mother Teresa

Many times people said to me at Whizz-Kidz, 'Surely the government provides mobility equipment for disabled children?' To which the answer is: they do occasionally, but in such small numbers as to be negligible. (They also provide a mobility allowance, which most hard-pressed parents use to buy a family car.)

The government, of whatever political persuasion, cannot keep pace with every pressing social, medical and cultural need because the only place to get such enormous resources from is us, the tax payers. Perceived wisdom, supported by many polls, shows that most of us want to pay less tax, not more. Often the only way to persuade government to support a particular cause is by lobbying the relevant powers skilfully, persistently and hard. Then real change can, and sometimes does, happen.

As our expectations continue to rise, the cost of meeting them rises with it. Today's parents expect computers, interactive teaching and internet access as part of their child's education. A newly qualified nurse has more medical knowledge than a doctor had 100 years ago. Those passionate about the arts want to ensure that access and opportunity is open to everyone, especially the young. In every area of life the investment needed today is enormous compared with that of even twenty years ago.

The government can and does provide money, but it is not that good at providing care, and, as Mother Teresa said, it doesn't usually offer love. It is the love that asks for no payback that gets things done.

> *If I speak in the tongues of men and of angels, but have not love, I am only a resounding gong or a clanging cymbal. If I have the gift of prophecy and can fathom all mysteries and all knowledge, and if I have a faith that can move mountains, but have not love, I am nothing. If I give all I possess to the poor and surrender my body to the flames, but have not love, I gain nothing. Love is patient, love is kind. It does not envy, it does not boast, it is not proud. It is not rude, it is not self-seeking, it is not easily angered, it keeps no record of wrongs. Love does not delight in evil but rejoices with the truth. It always protects, always trusts, always hopes, always perseveres.* 1 Corinthians, 1–13

The Fabric of Society

Charities, and charitable work, are part of the DNA of British society. Today, in every town and city throughout the country, most of the major national charities are represented, as well as many smaller local ones. They look after children who have been abused, women suffering from domestic violence, the elderly, the homeless, those with mental or physical disabilities, or with cancer, Parkinson's, multiple sclerosis and alzheimer's. Many others support animal welfare and environmental organisations.

To say nothing of people supporting the work of the National Trust, the RNLI and overseas aid charities such as the Red Cross and Oxfam. Many museums, arts and cultural organisations are also charities, for instance, the Tate, London Zoo, the Edinburgh Festival, the Royal Opera House, the Natural History Museum and many schools, churches and hospital trusts. There is a charity for every cause, and sometimes several charities supporting the same cause, caring for every possible social and physical need. All benefit from tax breaks and all actively fundraise in a variety of ways, including holding events, operating local shops, and enlisting the support of individuals and companies.

A great many people in your own community are formally or informally linked to one or more of these causes, daily carrying out thousands of acts of selfless caring and kindness, doing something useful to help other people, usually in addition to their day job. Quietly, on a regular basis and without making a fuss. A surprising number of your friends and work colleagues will be already involved in these organisations and doing this work: fundraising, helping out as a carer, acting as a trustee or governor, or just pitching in wherever they are needed.

And just as likely, someone you know is being looked after by someone working with a charity. Even though they may never tell you.

Who Gives to Charity?

Public donations to charity have remained at the same level for the past decade. Which is particularly sobering when you think about the overall increase in wealth some sections of society have enjoyed over the same period. (See Philanthropy page 142.)

Generosity is a life choice that seems to have very little connection with your income level.

Two out of three adults in Britain claim to give to charities every month. In 2005–6 the amount we gave came to £8.9 billion (with legacies the total is around £10 billion). It sounds a lot, until you compare it with the amount that we spend on other things every year, such as fast food and takeaways (£7.4 billion). Women are more likely to give than men, and people on lower incomes give a higher percentage of their earnings – 3 per cent – than people with good incomes, who only give 1 per cent. More is raised in total from the professional classes, because they earn more. One in twenty of us give more than £50 a month, and these people contribute an extraordinary 55.9 per cent of the total amount donated.

> You might have thought that British people give mostly to charities for animals and children, but surprisingly the top five causes are:
>
> - **international**
> - **cancer**
> - **religious – general services**

- heritage/environment
- arts/culture

(Charities Aid Foundation: Charity Trends, 2006)

Charity Facts

The charity sector is one of the largest 'industries' in Britain. It's huge. There are currently just over 190,000 registered charities in England and Wales (Scottish charities are registered separately). Of these, 168,000 are 'main' charities with 21,000 subsidiaries or branches. Their combined total annual income for 2006–7 was the equivalent of around 4 per cent of GDP, at over £41 billion. There's now a super-league of large charities. The National Trust currently has an income of around £337 million, Barnardo's £193 million and Cancer Research UK £423 million. These, and other organisations like them, are, in effect, large businesses.

The 627 biggest charities attract over 49 per cent of the total income. Take a broader perspective and 8 per cent receive a whopping 90 per cent. And these major players are successful in getting more from us – the public. Their average income saw a large increase in 2006–7, while averages for smaller charities fell.

The stated asset value of all charities is currently over £78 billion, but would be much higher if they were commercial organisations. Part of the art of managing a charity is not to make the balance sheet look too healthy in case your fundraisers disappear. Some charities write off all assets in the year of purchase, or write down the value of buildings and land owned 'because it will never be sold'.

Creative accounting.

At the other end of the scale, about four-fifths of charities have an annual income of £10,000 or less, and these receive less than 1 per cent of the total recorded income. They are usually started by a family or a local community to support a very specific aim, and run from a spare room with a group of committed volunteers. Though small, these organisations often achieve minor miracles.

Most charities are driven by passion. They take risks, push the boundaries and pilot new schemes that would be difficult for local or central government to contemplate. Often the government encourages this path-finding role and makes the necessary money available. In fact, the government is the largest source of charity funding, and outsources much of its work to charities.

Then it's down to us, the general public and second largest funder, to support our favourite charities through donations, volunteering, buying from charity shops, supporting fundraising events and leaving legacies.

According to the Charity Commission for England and Wales (Facts and Figures 2006; www.charity-comission.gov.uk), in 2006 there were over 600,000 paid employees, about 2.5 per cent of the total UK workforce, and 27 per cent of the population volunteered once a month, including fundraisers, front-line staff, carers and nurses. There were 900,000 charity trustees.

Why Do Charities Start?

I began Whizz-Kidz because I took up a personal challenge to help fund an electric wheelchair for a child with cerebral palsy. I did it to improve her independence and quality of life, and in doing so found that the reason she couldn't get about on her own was that government provision stretched only so far. Only when it was pointed out that there were thousands of other kids in a similar situation who had no proper mobility equipment or were using the wrong sort because they had been sold something they didn't need, did a group of friends decide to do something about it.

The really remarkable thing about it is that it isn't remarkable. It is the same for thousands of others – from the Anthony Nolan Foundation to Barnardo's. Charities are started because people see a need and do something about it. They aren't prepared to accept second best for their disabled child, for the relative suffering from Alzheimer's or for the friend whose life has been irreparably damaged by drug abuse. If we put a lid on the creation of new charities, we put a lid on their energy, creativity and commitment.

Individuals have created the charity industry. They are amongst Britain's truly great entrepreneurs. There will be at least 190,000 passionate people behind the 190,000 charities around today and they have one significant difference from the business entrepreneurs we read so much about. They are driven by passion not profit, by the desire to make a difference rather than money. Behind the creation of each charity you can nearly always find an inspiring story. Here are just some:

The Samaritans

This charity was started in 1953 by a young vicar called Chad Varah. Its name at the start was '999 for the suicidal'. He conducted a funeral for a fourteen-year-old girl who had taken her own life when her periods started, because she believed she had a sexually transmitted disease. As a result (and in an era when this was revolutionary) Chad began teaching sex education and counselling young couples. He then discovered that there were a disproportionately high number of suicides amongst young men and was given the opportunity to set up a counselling service for them.

They came in numbers far too great for him to see personally, so he recruited volunteers to give them cups of tea and sympathy until they could be ushered into his presence. But he came to understand that the tea and sympathy, the fact that someone was actually listening, resolved many of their problems. What people wanted us someone to listen uncritically, to give them space and make them feel less alone. Mother Teresa would have called it love.

Today the Samaritans operate over 200 UK centres manned by 230 volunteers for every member of staff. In prisons, prisoners are being trained as 'listeners'. In 2006, 1,700 trained prison volunteers supported over 90,000 fellow inmates. Text messaging is being piloted to reach younger people, and, without any significant promotion, has responded with 149,000 texts in under a year. An astonishing 5.2 million people in crisis contact the Samaritans each year in Britain and the Republic of Ireland. To connect with someone who will listen when they feel alone and desperate.

Barnardo's

Thomas Barnardo had set up a school in the East End of London for poor children to get a basic education. One day one of his pupils took him on a tour of the East End to show him how the children lived. They were sleeping on roofs and in gutters. The encounter so affected him he decided to devote himself to helping destitute children.

It was three years before he opened his first shelter in 1870, and he regularly went out at night into the slums to find destitute boys he could help. One evening an eleven-year-old called John Summers found his way to the shelter and asked to come in. He was turned away because the shelter was full. Two days later he was found dead from malnutrition and exposure. From then on Barnardo's bore the sign 'No Destitute Child Ever Refused Admission'.

Over 130 years later that one shelter has become 383 projects across Britain, and children's homes have been replaced by work with vulnerable children and their families, offering counselling, life-skills, adoption, fostering and more. It is one of the superleague of high-profile charities and helps over 110,000 kids and their families. It is an organisation which most of us take for granted.

Save the Children

This charity was the brainchild of Dorothy Buxton and Eglantyne Jebb. Horrified by the conditions of children who had survived the food shortages and blockades of the First World War, they set up the 'Fight the Famine Council' in 1919 to campaign for 'justice and compassion for the defeated nations'. Their aim was to raise money to send to children in European countries devastated by war.

Whilst Dorothy began to concentrate on political campaigning, Eglantyne led the creation of the Save the Children Fund. Today its mission is 'to fight for children's rights, and deliver immediate and lasting improvements to children's lives worldwide'.

In less than ninety years Save the Children has grown to operate in fifty-two countries, with 400 volunteer branches and 4,000 volunteers in the UK. The charity's income in 2005–6 was £163 million. All because two women saw a need and decided to do something about it.

The Anthony Nolan Bone Marrow Trust

Anthony Nolan was born in 1971, suffering from a rare bone disease which left his immune system unable to fight infection. His only hope of survival was a bone marrow transplant from a matching donor. At that time there was no register of potential donors, but his mother Shirley didn't let that stand in her way and launched a TV appeal during which her seven-year-old won the hearts of millions of viewers. When Anthony sadly died, his mother decided his short life should leave a legacy.

Today the Anthony Nolan Bone Marrow Trust's register of suitable donors has grown to 382,000 people; it carries out 12,000 searches for a tissue match a year and taps into global registers as well. Tissue-matching is complex but in 2006, 530 UK patients were treated thanks to the charity's efforts. Shirley Nolan died in 2003, but the legacy she left is a charity with an income of £17 million a year, offering life-saving treatment to more and more people. Chances that her son, Anthony, didn't have. What a legacy!

Amnesty International

Peter Berenson, a British lawyer, decided to start Amnesty

International after reading a newspaper article about two Portuguese students drinking a toast to liberty in a Lisbon restaurant, and being imprisoned. In May 1961 he wrote an article in the *Observer* newspaper called 'The Forgotten Prisoners'.

Over 1,000 people read the appeal to do something practical, such as lobbying for the students' release, and offering support for the idea of an international campaign to protect human rights. Today Amnesty is a worldwide movement with more than 1.8 million members who support its mission to prevent grave abuses of human rights.

Small Charities Need You!

Some charities find it a great deal easier to raise money for their cause than others. If I did a sponsored cycle ride for Whizz-Kidz, most people that I approached would sponsor me. But if I asked them to sponsor me to raise money to fund an addiction centre, or a domestic violence programme, I am quite certain people would be less forthcoming. Which is why I have chosen to profile here five smaller charities and causes that sometimes find getting support difficult. They are significant, because every one grew from an entrepreneurial spirit to act, not for glory or profit, but because it was the right thing to do.

The people who start or work in these organisations will tell you again and again that their life has been richer from the moment they decided to do something to address the injustice they felt, saw or experienced. You're unlikely to see them in the headlines, but they are the unsung heroes amongst us, people going quietly about their work showing tremendous commitment, energy, compassion, per-

Domestic Violence

For over a year Julia Pemberton repeatedly begged the police to protect her from her husband, who had threatened to kill her. On 18 November 2003 he forced his way into her home, shooting and killing her seventeen-year-old son William and then Julia, as she crouched terrified in a cupboard, on the phone to the local police. Her last moments, begging for help, were poignantly recorded in a sixteen-minute tape played at her inquest. Her husband then shot himself.

A woman gets out of the boot of a car in a busy high street. Concerned that she may have been kidnapped, passers-by approach her and ask if she is OK. Yes, she replies, I always go to work in the boot of the car because my husband doesn't like me talking on the way to work.

Another woman moves with her children to a new town for the third time in a year. Police identify her ex-partner's car driving around near her home. A knife is dropped through her letterbox. She says to police: 'I might as well give up'. I know he will kill me. I can't move my children again.'

Domestic violence is 'living in fear of physical abuse or the anguish of mental control'. Every minute of every day the police receive a phone call from a woman who has been subjected to domestic violence, and on average a woman is assaulted thirty-five times before she makes the call.

> In the UK domestic violence kills two women every week, and accounts for 60% of female murders in the UK. Nine out of ten reported cases never reach court.

Diana Barran had a successful career in the City, and then changed direction joining New Philanthropy Capital, a charity that assesses charities on behalf of a new breed of wealthy donor. She had given grants to three children's charities, when she paused to ask the managers of each of them what they considered to be the most pressing social issue affecting their children. Each one said domestic violence. After researching the area she discovered that huge strides had been made in the provision of refuges. Her focus was to try and keep women and children safe in their homes. Diana built on the best practice from the US and the UK to offer specialist support to women while harnessing the authority of all the statutory agencies with a single focus: safety. She created a new charity, **CAADA (Coordinated Action Against Domestic Violence)**, and a new group of Independent Domestic Violence Advocates (IDVAs) trained to throw a safety net round the woman, coordinating all the necessary agencies in the area – the police, probation and social services, the courts, A&E, locksmiths etc – into so-called 'MARACs' (Multi-Agency Risk Assessment Conferencing). In South Wales, the work of the IDVAs has enabled 70 per cent of their clients to live free from either physical or emotional abuse, and there has been a significant fall in related deaths.

There are now 275 such advocates. Each one can support seventy women and, as a consequence, CAADA is able to defend over 19,000 women and around 30,000 children a year. In the next five years the charity aims to have trained 1,200 IDVAs and established 300 MARACs to address the safety of 100,000 people who urgently need help.

As an example of what one person can achieve with vision and determination, Diana's work is a hard act to beat. And as a 'return on investment' it has been startlingly effective. A charity formed in only December 2004, with a total expenditure to date of just over £1 million, has informed and improved Home Office policy on domestic violence and saved the lives of many women. Diana is one of those remarkable women who 'get things done' with a lethal combination of energy, intelligence and a very large dollop of charm. Her motivation has developed from an original 'intellectual analysis': that there was a much better and more effective way to provide support for victims of domestic violence.

Now she is as driven by the impact on the children, as 70 per cent of children taken into care have experienced domestic violence. Diana says, 'This is the price we pay for not sorting it out. Reading the analysis after a child has been killed or seriously injured just makes you want to cry. There is so much we can do to avoid these cases.'

CAADA
P.O. Box 4065
Bruton
Somerset BA10 0WX
Tel: 01749 812968
→ www.caada.org.uk

The Environment

I can't add much more to this extract from an online interview by *American Scientist* with Lester R. Brown, author of *Plan B 2.0: Rescuing a Planet Under Stress and a Civilization in Trouble* (Norton, 2006). It says it all:

> The oil peak, water shortages and global warming are related in the sense that they are all driven by the enormous growth in world population and economic activity. With oil we are depleting a resource that is not renewable in a relevant human time frame. Water shortages are the result of ever-growing demands for water, primarily to produce food. Global warming is the result of the enormous growth in the use of fossil fuels and the associated rise in carbon emissions to the point where they exceed the Earth's capacity to absorb them ...
>
> If China one day has three cars for every four people, US-style, it will have 1.1 billion cars. The whole world today has 800 million cars. To provide the roads, highways and parking lots to accommodate such a vast fleet, China would have to pave an area equal to the land it now plants in rice. It would need 99 million barrels of oil a day. Yet the world currently produces 84 million barrels per day and may never produce much more ...
>
> If a few years from now it were to become clear that the arctic ice melting is indeed going to lead to the melting of the Greenland ice sheet and that we cannot save it, then we may face, for the first time in history, a fracturing of societies along generational lines. We have experienced social fracturing along racial, religious and ethnic lines, but never before along generational lines. The next gener-

ation, which will have to cope with the rise in sea level that we have set in motion, will be asking us why we did not act. How, they will ask, could you do this to us? They will be able to read the same scientific literature and the warnings from the scientific community that we now read ...

Watch Al Gore's film, *An Inconvenient Truth*, buy Lester Brown's book, and start visiting a few websites – Friends of the Earth is a good place to begin (www.foe.co.uk) and, if you are feeling complacent, www.worldometers.info. Also www.earth-policy.org . The overall message is that the world in which our children are growing up and will live in is going to be very different, very soon. As in the next couple of decades. But if we all get our act together now, the issues of climate change, over-population, food and water shortages, desertification, changes in biodiversity and more could be tackled. In fact, they <u>must</u> be tackled.

The current world population is 6.6 billion people. By 2050 it is likely to be 9 billion. If you have grasped the fact that the environment is one, if not the most important challenge, facing us, and want to know what you can do, then read on.

The busy, popular Tony Juniper is the CEO of **Friends of the Earth**. He arrives for our interview having just passed an advertisement in the street for an online travel company, promoting five holiday trips abroad a year. This, at a time when even the dimmest person on the planet has heard that flying is not all that good for the environment! *Air travel* is growing at 6 per cent to 8 per cent a year, which is completely unsustainable, and 'the UK government' of any political persuasion subsidises air travel to the tune of a £9 billion a year tax break, through not taxing fuel at the same level as cars, not charging VAT on the servicing of aircraft, not applying air passenger duty. On top of that, the commercial drive to expand airports and increase capacity is in direct conflict with plans to save carbon emissions. The market, yet again, is trumping policy, though Tony has noticed a surprising culture change has started where it is now acceptable to discuss different ways of travel, taking holidays, air miles and food miles openly in a way that might well lead to real change in five years time. Some offset schemes do make a difference but most are nonsense. We have come to regard £10 flights abroad almost as a human right. This in spite of the fact that 80 per cent of all aircraft take-off and landings are in Europe. Many of these journeys could easily be switched to travelling by train, and would take the same time or be quicker. There are sixty planes to Paris each day and thirty-seven to Manchester from London alone.

As for long-distance air travel, if you have or want to go to Australia or India, the message is: just fly less and think about it more.

> A return flight to Australia generates 2,325kg CO^2 per passenger (source: 'Fly Now Grieve Later' by Brendon Sewill, Aviation Environment Federation).
>
> If 3.2kg CO^2 is emitted per litre of aviation kerosene, the amount of fuel used per passenger to Australia and back is 726.6 litres.
>
> If fuel tax were applied at the same rate as car fuel tax (48.35p per litre) it would add £351.31 to a return ticket.

What about **GM crops**? In a world facing severe food shortages isn't it a good idea? To which his answer is that the whole debate is an irrelevance, Juniper claims it doesn't actually work, all sorts of claims have been made and most have been exposed as hype, with some bordering on immoral as companies use the issue of food security to get farmers hooked into their products.

Climate change? Tony is justifiably proud of the Climate Bill going through Parliament calling for a new law to make annual cuts in carbon dioxide. It was created by Friends of the Earth and supported by over 130,000 people (all on a budget of just £35,000).

China? The big question for many people in the UK is: 'What is the point of us changing our lightbulbs if they are in a period of huge industrial and technological expansion?'

Tony's answer is this: 'In the West we have strong economies already, and therefore the space and the capacity to do something about it. And we are responsible for most of the carbon dioxide that is up there already and causing the trouble. So these nations are saying, "Why should we slow down our economic growth when you who caused it and have the capacity to do something about it aren't doing so?" The West needs to set an example and show that we are going low carbon and that we can maintain a high level of economic welfare whilst providing a high level of comfort for our own people. If China and India see that we can sustain a happy, vibrant and effective economy by changing our ways they might well follow ...'

So what can we do? 'We have two key and important roles, where we really can affect change. One is the way we use our vote. We should only vote for people who understand and are committed to the environment change. Politicians will act when they think the public are interested in the issue. The second is the way we choose to spend our own money. This includes everything from seeking out more environmentally friendly methods of transport to buying our food from local producers. Why buy butter from New Zealand, milk from Holland and carrots from South Africa when we can produce these ourselves, and save our farms and farmland? Ultimately, political change, marketing and public attitudes must work together.'

Friends of the Earth
26–28 Underwood Street,
London N1 7JQ
Tel: 0207 490 1555
→ www.foe.co.uk

TWELVE THINGS TO DO FOR THE ENVIRONMENT

1. Buy less stuff – do you really need it?
2. Choose local food and shop locally.
3. Measure your carbon footprint (www.actonco2.direct.gov.uk). Aim to reduce it.
4. Switch to energy-efficient lightbulbs. They cost more but save up to £65 over their lifetime (up to ten years).
5. Boil the amount of water you need in a kettle – don't just fill it up.
6. Cycle or walk instead of using a car or public transport.

7. Use your vote. Only vote for people who understand and are committed to environmental issues.
8. Boycott plastic bags – take your own.
9. Watch the water you use carefully – shower instead of bathing.
10. Buy an environmentally friendly car.
11. Recycle. Just do it. The average person in the UK throws out their own bodyweight every three months.
12. Join Friends of the Earth and get their email newsletter.

(Source: Save Cash and Save the Planet, Collins, 2005)

Difficult Young People

The Greenhouse Schools Project works with disadvantaged children and young people in some of the most deprived areas of inner London. Their mission is to introduce them to sport and arts programmes that make a difference to their lives, their social skills, their self-respect and discipline. Greenhouse shows them how to respect others and how to work constructively as a team. They keep them off the streets and give them something positive in their lives.

In the first five months of 2007, six teenagers in London died in tragic circumstances – murdered in their homes or on their local streets. Five of the six victims attended schools at which Greenhouse regularly works; four of the victims were known to the charity personally and were participating in their sports programmes.

On an estate in North Peckham, close to where Damilola Taylor was murdered, 60 per cent of pupils in the local schools come from one parent families, 75 per cent qualify for free lunches, fewer than 10 per cent achieve five GCSE passes. Gangs, guns and drugs are part of the fabric of the area. It is here that Abdullah Ben Kmayal – known simply as Ben – has been teaching young people football for sixteen years. He is a true 'pied piper', and says if they weren't playing football and, more to the point, training to get into the team on Saturday, they would be 'lolling about' on the streets and some of them would be causing trouble.

Fatlum came to London from Albania aged eight and was soon known to the police. Unable to speak English, he was rarely in school and regularly in trouble, then he found the Greenhouse Schools table tennis programme. Now he is one of the top players in the country for his age, a regional champion aiming to represent Britain in the 2012 Olympics. A talent with a ping pong ball has transformed his education too, turning him into a star pupil and gifted linguist.

This summer 1,000 young people are taking part in 100 projects, including fourteen full-time table tennis programmes, dance, drama, basketball, dodgeball and more.

The man who created this remarkable charity is charming, focused and mad keen on sport. When Michael de Giorgio successfully sold his business in his early forties he used the same energy and management acumen he had used to build up his company to start a charity introducing young people from disadvantaged backgrounds to sport.

One day he noticed that the wonderful facilities in his son's school, St Paul's, were unused during the school holidays. In the summer of 2002, with the support of the headmaster and help and encouragement of a young local police officer, he and a friend created a fortnight of sports for some of the disadvantaged young people living in and around Barnes. The Greenhouse Schools Project was born.

Mike believes that participation in sport provides young people with goals, teaches them the importance of teamwork, how to win and how to lose, how to behave properly on the pitch or court, plus less obvious things, such as time-keeping, self-discipline, showing respect, and critically that you must train hard to play well. Many of the skills learned are transferable to other areas of work and life. And while sport attracts them in, once trust is established they talk to their coaches, deliberately chosen for their communication skills and 'coolness' about many other issues. A fourteen-year-old girl told her coach she was pregnant even before she told her parents.

Mike is a remarkably charming person, but not far beneath the surface lurks a clear determination to get things done. And not far beneath that is a very diffident and shy man. At the end of our interview I asked him why he started Greenhouse and what other forms of charity he was engaged in. He volunteered 'a sense of responsibility to help others', 'a Catholic sense of guilt', a feeling that he was fortunate, an ability to talk to potential funders ... and then ground to an embarrassed halt. I knew he did more, but decided to leave him in peace.

Greenhouse Schools Project
G2 Shepherds Studios
Rockley Road
London W14 0DA
Tel: 0207 603 5111
→ www.greenhouseschools.org

Counselling for Children

These are some of the problems encountered in a London primary school (Year 6, children aged ten and eleven) during a recent two-year period. This list may come as a bit of a shock:

- Two guns brought onto site.
- Mobile phone stealing ring.
- Children bullying by text and MSN Messenger.
- Happy slapping.
- Children involved in stealing and bad behaviour on buses.
- Children involved in jumping on and off trains at railway station.
- One child involved in pushing someone under a train.
- A boy getting girls to strip for him over the internet.
- A boy taking £2,000 and handing out £50 notes in the playground.
- Parents fighting – one stabbed, one had finger bitten off.
- Parents verbally and physically abusing other people's children.
- One parent running another over outside school, deliberately.
- Stealing.
- One girl went missing – taken into a car by four men – and was never heard of again. The mother was complicit.
- One girl drove her mother's car, took her mother's money and drugs, and was being used by pimps, whom the mother requested bring her to and from school.
- Year 6 girls (aged ten and eleven) wearing hipsters, thongs and fishnets.

THE MORE YOU GIVE, THE MORE YOU GET

Talking to Benny Refson about The Place2be, the charity she founded to provide a voice for primary school children, is inspiring. She is fun, full of energy and formidable. And the work that the charity does is like taking a trip into another almost Dickensian Britain. At our first meeting we both 'lose it' about the people we still meet who claim there are no poor people in Britain. (Even writing this annoys me!) Stories emerge of:

- Two brothers who steal money to buy food – crisps, usually – because their mother uses all her income to feed a drug habit. And there are no eating utensils in the home anyway.
- A child who cuts her wrists, 'mirroring' the behaviour of her mother who is a manic depressive.
- A little girl who saw her mother stabbed in front of her in the school playground.
- The children who didn't take part in a schools healthy eating initiative – everyone gets a free apple – because they had never seen fruit at home and their teeth were too bad.
- The boy of seven who attempted to hang himself in the school playground – his single mother had become a crack addict.

Benny's 'aha' moment came when she was counselling students between the ages of eighteen and twenty-five. They came to see her in enormous distress – and their problems could all be traced back to their early childhood. She realised that if she could work with younger children, they might be able to avoid the sense of hopelessness they encountered so often later in life.

So, with formidable determination, she founded The Place2be to provide counselling to children at primary schools throughout the UK. It's the background of the children that loads the dice against them.

In a Greenwich primary school with 400 pupils, the staff told me about the tremendous value in having The Place2Be office in the school where the children could go and talk about their worries and lives to someone who wasn't a teacher. The Place2Be staff highlighted some of the problems they faced on a day-to-day basis; two mothers talked about how valuable they had found the service for their children – one spoke movingly about how she had been the victim of domestic violence but was determined to make a new life for herself and her children; and five of the children spoke bravely about the value of having someone to go to talk to about 'life' at The Place2Talk's lunch-time drop-in service. Issues addressed at these meetings included domestic violence, criminality at home, child abuse, loss and bereavement, transitions, anger management, low self-esteem, parental relationship breakdown, witnessing violence and even murder.

The Place2Be's staff also work with parents, teachers and teaching assistants in the schools and ensure their work links up with that of other local agencies who work with the children. They work in 114 schools and with 37,000 children throughout the UK. These children are our future. As the Jesuits said: 'Give us the boy and we will give you the man.'

The Place2Be
Wapping Telephone Exchange
Royal Mint Street
London E1 8LQ Tel: 020 7780 6189
→ www.theplace2be.org.uk

CASE STUDY

Child: male, ten years of age

The boy is below height and weight for his age. His appearance is unkempt. His clothes appear unwashed and he is often smelling of urine as a result of his enuresis. Numerous appointments have been made for him to attend the enuresis clinic but these have not been attended.

It has been noted that he has worn the same uniform for weeks at a time which was identified due to the stains on the clothes being the same throughout this period. The child has also been unable to join in games lessons as he didn't own a PE kit. Children's Services provided money for two pairs of trousers and also £15 towards two school jumpers. Although a slight improvement was noticed, with the child wearing new trousers, he is still without new jumpers.

At the age of six he was caught numerous times stealing food from other children's lunchboxes because he was so hungry. He often cried if he could not have seconds. At that time it was also recorded that he was small and wet the bed. Currently he often wants to eat his lunch early as he cannot last until lunchtime due to his hunger.

The child told the school that he was allowed free school dinners. It transpired that he was getting his dinner money from home but keeping the money in order to buy toys.

The above issues cause the child great distress. He has talked about being called names by his peers, about how his peers refuse to sit next to him due to his body odour. He has also talked about showering every day but has stated that there is no money for shower gel or soap. Given his general appearance and body odour it is questionable if he has a shower at all. When a member of school staff asked him what was the most important thing in his life, he said, 'Nothing.'

His family home shows signs of extreme deprivation. All the windows are boarded up except in the kitchen. One of the boards covering the window to the child's bedroom was broken and unsecured for a long period of time. The house is like a building site with tools lying around and work on-going. There is no bedding on the beds and no sign of toys for any of the three children.

Addiction

'Society' isn't sympathetic to addicts, or the problems caused by addiction. In our society, being 'in control' is important and highly valued. Being 'out of control' is stigmatising. Paradoxically, people are drawn to certain substances and behaviours because they seem to promise a beguiling measure of control (the fix) over feelings: relief, relaxation, disinhibition, insulation, excitement, arousal, escape, power. It is more difficult for people to own up to an addiction than many other medical condition. It is often viewed as a weakness, or at best a character failing, and a person with an addiction is seen as 'self-destructing'. And yet the psychology of addiction is complex, the scope of it is broad, and the problems it causes pervade every part of our lives:

- Addiction is the number one cause of preventable death in the UK.
- Substance addiction alone takes a toll of about 138,000 lives a year.
- 70 per cent of all crime is drug-related.
- Alcohol is a factor in 90 per cent of child abuse cases.
- One in five secondary school children between the ages of eleven and fifteen have tried drugs in the last twelve months.
- Smoking-related illnesses costs the NHS a fortune.

When I meet Tristan Millington-Drake and Nick Barton at the offices of **Action on Addiction** one of my first questions is: 'How do you recognise that you are addicted?'

There are several signs or clues. One is 'loss of control'. The experience of a person who is addicted is that they haven't got any control. They are lost. And the loss of control is *over* the substance or behaviour. This is characteristic of addiction, as is the struggle to regain it. Repeated relapse after attempts to stop is also a key sign. Another is the development of an all-consuming relationship with the substance or behaviour concerned. You can be in a business meeting or having a conversation with a friend but your mind is elsewhere: in the fridge or betting shop; where you will get your next drink, or place your next bet.

Your mind starts to narrow in focus, your relationship with the substance or behaviour starts to become exclusive and it takes over your life. You can't do without it. There is a state of dependency. As this dependency gets worse the addict's consciousness of their addiction gets less, but the people around him notice the impact much more. The addict becomes secretive and deluded, in effect entering into a love affair with the drug or behaviour which is very intense and potentially fatal. All addictions have an obsessive or compulsive quality.

And there is a conflict, in that one part of an addict knows it is harmful yet he or she strives to continue his or her relationship with the addiction.

Tristan recalls a male client who hadn't drunk for a year, then went on a bender and landed up in a prison cell before coming to treatment: 'I asked him what made him give up drink for a year. And his answer was: "Everyone got on my case, my employer, my family, my wife, and I was going to lose my job. I was very angry and defiant. I was determined to show them that I could go without a drink to get them off my back."' Tristan then asked him why he had gone back to drinking after the year, to which the reply was: "The only thing that kept me going was the thought of the drink on day 365." His drinking had stopped but the problems underlying his addiction had stayed with him.

The perception that alcoholics or drug addicts are weak-willed is misplaced. Actually, there is no one more strong-willed than an alcoholic who wants a drink or a drug addict who wants a drug. They are very focused, almost psychopathic. All they want is the substance that makes them feel better again, which is why they will steal from family and friends.

This is the major irony. We do these things because they make us feel good not because they make us feel bad, but they become the problem rather than the solution.

There is also withdrawal. If you stop indulging in a particular habit, and go into some kind of physical or psychological withdrawal, then you recognise there *was* some kind of dependence. An addiction such as smoking is not only utterly compulsive, it also has a chemical factor which means an addict has an increased physical tolerance and therefore needs more nicotine to get the same effect.

The first requirement is that a person has to want to do something about the problem. The conflict and suffering has become too much, and the consequences of carrying on in the same way are hugely damaging. Intervention can often help: an addict might go into treatment as a result of pressure in the workplace or from family, and the results can be good. Another trigger is some outside factor that hits hard, a doctor telling an addict he or she is going to die.

Every addict's desire is to control their addiction – not to have it control them. So asking for the help rather than trying to do it solo is another key step. This help could come via their GP, counsellor, individual therapist or self-help group such as Alcoholics Anonymous (AA). There isn't a right or wrong place to start. What *is* important is that the help must be skilled, and very often it isn't, which is why Action on Addiction is setting up the Centre for Addiction Treatment Studies.

For several years Tristan and Nick had been talking about bringing together key addiction charities. In March 2007 they succeeded, merging the Chemical Dependency Centre, Clouds and Action on Addiction into one charity. Their aim is to 'disarm addiction' by understanding how best to respond to the problem and treat it successfully.

They face several problems, one of which is that the majority of their income is statutory (i.e. government funded). It is not a popular area with the public so never gets the attention it deserves.

As Nick says: 'We are actually put in the same position as the addict, anxiously deprived, looking for a little money here and there, our "hit" to do our vital work ... It would be good to be able to get on with the job rather than constantly searching for funds.' One of their key areas of focus is to be on the 1.3 million children living with addicted parents. They are currently developing a national programme called Moving Parents and Children Together (M-PACT).

Some final words from a recovering addict: 'An unfortunate side effect of being addicted to alcohol is that one becomes a liar and very deceitful, whether you are secretly stuffing your face with chocolate, sleeping with every man in the UK, buying 500 pairs of shoes on your credit card, or pouring bottles and bottles of wines and spirits down your neck ... Addiction takes you to extremes. Boundaries are crossed, people are hurt, lives destroyed, but does the addict care? Not on your nelly. They care about the next drink, spliff, line, chocolate bar, exercise class. The fix they need to make them feel better about themselves and the world around them. Then it goes too far and you don't even care about the world around you or the people in it.'

And later:

'Then, eighteen months ago, I was given a moment of clarity. I reached my rock bottom. I called for help and got it in the form of a twelve-step programme of recovery. Life has changed incredibly, circumstances have improved and things are happening beyond my wildest dreams. I have met a man who I love very much indeed. My children love me, and I love and care for them and am really there for them. We do stuff now instead of all staying in the house whilst I drink myself into oblivion.'

Action on Addiction
Head Office
East Knoyle
Salisbury
Wiltshire SP3 6BE
Tel: 01747 830 733
→ www.actiononaddiction.org.uk

Charity Management

'I want every pound that I give to charity to go directly to the cause.' Those of us who have been privileged to work in the charity sector have had to put up with this nonsense for many years, and still do.

Charities have to be efficiently run. They are complex organisations that should be as accountable to the people who support them as to the people and causes they help. They must be managed as professionally as any business, because, frankly, they make a more important contribution to the quality of this nation's life than most business or commercial enterprises. In simple terms, they matter more.

Helping people who are vulnerable is important work, which needs proper funding and skilful management. The people who help to care for a friend, support your father's Parkinson's with great patience and love, who offer refuge to women who are being beaten up, or a lifeline to children who are being abused, who struggle to provide food for thousands dying of starvation or AIDS every week in Africa – they all have to know what they are doing and do it very well. I have watched many such people caring for others with a gentleness and love that is genuinely humbling. If you are one of these saints you are an absolute blessing and an example to the rest of us.

Volunteers are wonderful, but it is unfair and otherworldly to expect charities to be managed by them, to believe that all the money raised will magically appear at no cost, that someone will pick up the tab for the phone, the printing, the postage, the office rent, the computer equipment, the training, the accounting. It's not a world we would tolerate. Within days of the 2004 tsunami disaster all of the major aid charities were in action, which they could only do because they had professionals managing the giving in England and assessing the programme on the ground. Well-intentioned volunteers, however talented, could never co-ordinate something on this scale. It may be natural to wish that every penny we give would go straight to the beneficiaries, and that there are no overheads, but only a moment's thought will tell us it's managerial nonsense.

At last, influential people in government, some grant-making trusts and, increasingly, enlightened wealthy individuals are starting to recognise that core administration and management costs need proper subsidy. They fund new projects and initiatives supported by a business plan, in which the impact or outcomes are clearly explained and where there is a sum of money specifically set aside for its successful management.

Whizz-Kidz received a number of different grants from one of the major charitable trusts, Henry Smith, each of which funded a new initiative. The first funded our first children's therapist. Another funded our first director of children's services; and another our first information officer, a post created to collect all the information available about children's mobility issues and make it available to clinical professionals, parents, MPs, civil servants at the department of health, and the children themselves. A truly productive partnership with a thoughtful trust.

> ### HOW DO CHARITIES GIVE VALUE FOR MONEY?
>
> David Robinson, founder of Community Links and the We Are What We Do movement, is a remarkable man. A quiet person who listens and then inspires others to action, he made the point clearly:
> 'For years I could look out of our office window early in the morning, across the market, to the queue outside the Post Office. It wasn't open at that time but already pensioners, single people, mothers with children were waiting for their benefit payment. Our sponsors could take the money that they'd been giving us, convert it all into used fivers and hand out bundles in the queue. It would bring immediate comfort, relief and joy. It could be a worthwhile thing to do. Doing otherwise required Community Links to do better. To make a legitimate case for their money, we had to prove that we could add to the value of the fiver and bring greater benefit to that queue. We might be running training, or producing publications, or delivering other services remote from the frontline. In the end the money must have a measurable impact on the proverbial queue and the impact must amount to more than could be achieved with the straightforward distribution of cash.'

Chief Executives

Charity chief executives are paid less than they would be for doing a similar role in the commercial sector, and they have very different measures of success. In the commercial world, success is measured comparatively easily by the amount of profit generated – the bottom line. On the other hand, running an organisation with a social ethos, and staffed by people whose main aim is to help others, can be a different order of management challenge.

In charities, the main measure of success is the impact that your organisation has each year in the area in which you work. This might be bringing about a change in government policy or generating more calls to your helpline as much as providing more direct help to your users.

The RNID – Royal National Institute for the Deaf – pioneered a new kind of reporting under its then chief executive, James Strachan. Each year the charity sets out what it intends to achieve in each area of its work, and in the following year in an annual review it reports on how it has done. The financial information still has an important spot but is no longer the lead. This approach is now a requirement in the way charities present their annual report.

A good CEO has to select, employ and motivate people to help the cause and its constituents, while paying lower salaries than these people could earn in the marketplace. Done well this leads to a highly motivated group of people, who tend to choose their jobs because they have a different value system.

At Whizz-Kidz I tried to follow Robert Greenleaf's management model of servant leadership, where the leader sets the values and the vision and then makes sure the employees have everything needed to do their jobs. In such an environment you have to inspire the people in every area of work to drive the organisation forward and include them as much as possible in the decision-making process so that they really do have ownership of the charity.

One of my best moments at Whizz-Kidz was when a confidential staff survey indicated that approval ratings for enjoyment of work, pride in the charity, belief and involvement in the management all got marks well into 90 per cent. Everyone had tremendous belief in the charity, enjoyed working for it and believed that they were contributing to the growth of the organisation.

Financial Management

Forecasting income for a charity is difficult. Imagine how difficult it would be to plan sensibly for a business with little guaranteed income that has to invent new income generating activities every year. Planning for long-term survival against the fickleness of public donations, the whims of changing government priorities and economic uncertainty is a challenge. People may give for a new project – to build a special needs facility, open a day care centre, create a new service initiative – but when the building is complete, and the new service requires continuing money to keep the show on the road, pay the staff to deliver that service, and maintain the building, they lose interest. But if the running costs cannot be covered on a sound basis, regular crises will occur. Shutting down a day care centre for the elderly, or a residential home for the blind, is in a different league to closing a poorly performing part of a commercial business. Some work cannot have an exit date.

As a result, charity's finances have to be managed carefully. Smaller ones have to manage their growth without borrowing, whilst at the same time trying to build up small reserves. Ask any tiny charity about their 'reserves policy' and you will usually be met with a huge guffaw. Too busy working to fill in the funding application forms, or set up a successful fundraising event, and struggling 24/7 to do the work they are set up to do, it is a very hard act to pull off.

We made it a rule at Whizz-Kidz never to have an overdraft, and our reserves policy was to accumulate three months worth of the charity's annual overhead, to be used in case of hard times. At the same time we were funding the charity's growth to meet increasing demands. What this meant in practice was saving a small proportion of the income each month and ring-fencing it, rather than spending it on equipment for children, or the salary for a new member of staff. Sure enough, there was a year when income was below forecast and the trustees were able to use some of the reserves to make up the shortfall, otherwise there would have been cuts in services or staff.

For a few charities this is not a problem. It is a well-known fact within the charity sector that some of the largest and best known charities in the country do not need any more money. Their reserves are enormous, and their reasons to exist are not of the same importance as when they were originally formed, however much they protest about possible future 'rainy days'. If you think you are supporting one of these charities, see if it has enough money in its reserves or investments to continue its work for several years ahead, and if so stop supporting it. You donate your money to charity to be used, not invested on the stock market. Look for the total amount of its annual income over the past few years to take into account any unusual or one-off large donations of funds. Compare this with their total annual expenditure. With luck one should approximately equal the other. Now 'ook at their reserves, including investments, and work out how long the charity could continue to do its work, if it took no money for six months, a year or even two.

It is, however, important to distinguish between these charities and grant-making trusts whose reserves are invested to fund many future years of annual grants.

Raising Money

You are probably more aware of the charities that rely on public fundraising rather than government funding because public profile is essential to get donations flowing.

Raising money for a charity, as anyone who has done it will tell you, is difficult. Fundraising for a living is an extremely challenging and competitive occupation, and good fundraisers are like gold dust. While some charities will collaborate on the work with clients and lobbying, even combining back office facilities to work more efficiently, competition between fundraisers is fierce.

It costs money to raise money. Why this should be a surprise to most people escapes me. All events cost money, and it is hoped that they will cover those costs and make a good profit for the charity. It takes knowledge and persistence to complete an application to a trust or a government body for a major grant (with government often requiring a competitive tendering process where competing organisations bid against each other for work), and the energy and commitment of several members of staff to get the most out of a charity partnership with a large company.

Fundraising is now a career, but still paid less than would be the norm in the commercial sector, and without pay incentives and year end bonuses. The men and women who dream up increasingly inventive methods of raising money to 'sell' you their cause are in competition with other charities and everyone else for the remains of your disposable income.

Unlike campaigns to sell commercial and consumer products, such as cars, computers, toiletries and fashion, charities raise money, for the most part, without the backing of major advertising, marketing or public relations campaigns.

Communications and PR

Communications teams in charities have a challenging time. Championing the cause of disabled people, haemophiliacs, one-parent families or trying to persuade the general public to care about people dying in Africa is difficult.

Especially with minimum resources. As with their fundraising colleagues, they usually have to 'blag' pro bono support from PR and advertising agencies. Fortunately, many of these agencies seem instinctively to understand that their day job is unlikely to change the world and generously give their time and talents. The impact of a highly creative group of people working on a campaign can be huge, such as the short films made for the Make Poverty History campaign.

It's Not All Good News

As in all areas of work and life, there are some charities which don't operate as effectively as they could or should do.

Some of the larger organisations are as conservative, slow-moving and bureaucratic as the government departments from whom many receive considerable funds. When a significant part of your income comes through government contracts it is hard not to become submerged in a bureaucratic mindset. In effect, these charities are recycling government money, often in a pretty ineffective way, to meet targets rather than change lives. Even the staff in these organisations have 'lost the will to live' because it can take months, sometimes years, to get a simple and straightforward decision taken.

Very often charity management is third-rate, with no proper accountability to stakeholders. The trustees, who are unpaid and don't work in the charity, hold all the executive authority, and the organisation as a whole is unused to measuring outcomes in any sensible and persuasive manner. Many have no clear idea of where they are going and what success looks like. It can sometimes be quite hard to break through the 'we are doing good' ethos and ask difficult questions about what is actually being achieved.

Charities are also open to fraud. The student selling flowers for charity in your local pub may actually be genuine – accepting a low commission with the belief that they're doing good work – but the flower wholesalers give little, if any, of the profit away. A group of Whizz-Kidz fundraisers once told me that they were having a post-work drink when they were approached by someone selling roses and claiming to be raising money for – Whizz-Kidz!

And there are some charities doing similar work that really should merge their efforts, but don't. I know of at least two separate cases where this hasn't happened because the organisations concerned 'don't get on', and one that failed because of a real difference in their culture. On the other hand, the two largest cancer research charities – Cancer Research UK and the Imperial Cancer Research Fund – recently merged, and two other children's cancer charities – Sargent Cancer Care and CLIC – have joined together to form CLIC Sargent. So it can be done.

Starting Your Own Charity

Changing the world is fun, but first a 'government health warning'!

If you are by now so completely inspired to do something useful that you have decided that you are going to start a charity, PAUSE.

You are about to enter a world which has all the challenges of running a small business, without any control over the income and non-executive directors (trustees) who have all the executive authority without 'ownership' of the entity.

There also is a very strong chance that the work you want to do is already being carried out by an organisation set up to do just the same. It might make sense to join them. There is nothing to be gained by reinventing the wheel; it just makes other people's work more difficult. And however enthusiastic or dynamic you are, you actually don't know yet that you can run a charity, do you? Before we started Whizz-Kidz, we held a meeting with some of the largest disability charities in Britain and asked them what they thought of the idea of establishing a new charity to fund children's wheelchairs and other mobility equipment. Was anyone else doing it? Would they help us? They were enthusiastic and encouraged us to go ahead.

This book is to inspire you to be helpful and useful, not necessarily to start a new charity. That said, if you want to do it – good on you. As one of the co-founders of a charity I applaud your ambition. Most of the charities in this country were started by individual entrepreneurs who saw a need and filled it. I can assure you your life will be enriched beyond measure by working with people who will help you to see life from a different perspective.

Here are my top pragmatic hints for starting a successful charity – or at least avoiding making a complete Horlicks of it:

- When you've worked out what you think you want to do, go first to the Charity Commissioners (www.charity-commission.gov.uk). They have a unit to offer advice and make sure you don't fall at the first hurdle.
- Pay attention to what goes into your governance document. You may think you know exactly what you want to achieve, but if your goal is too narrow you could run into problems later. It's all very well supporting orphans in a single postal code area, but if your fundraising is successful you might not be able to spend all the money there. Be crystal clear what your governance responsibilities are and how in practical terms you are going to fulfil them.
- Think of a decent name to describe or illustrate the work you are doing. Using initials may seem clever but will be unfathomable to most people. You don't want to waste time explaining the acronym when you could be selling your work.

- Choose decent trustees, good-hearted people who have a relevant talent and time to help, not just people who are around or want to do it. Meet monthly. Small organisations are especially fragile, they need nurturing and constant monitoring. Actually, so do the larger charities, but they have somehow convinced themselves that they can monitor the organisation effectively by meeting quarterly.
- Don't have too many trustees. Avoid large boards like the plague. They are unmanageable and can be ineffective, political beyond belief, or even a mixture of both. Small groups that know each other well will take decisions at a proper pace.
- Start monthly management accounts from day one. Absolutely essential for reminding you about the true state of the organisation's finances as opposed to your 'hoped for version'.
- Measure what you're doing from day one. 'We've helped lots of elderly people' isn't specific enough to get new funding from a trust. They'll want to know how many people and the difference you made.
- Learn the difference between restricted and unrestricted funds. Restricted funds are those give to the charity for a specific purpose or project. Unrestricted funds can be used for anything within your charitable remit – those core costs that are difficult to fund like wages, or rent. You *must* account for these monies separately and you *must not* mix them up, such as borrowing from the project funds to pay wages. (All too tempting when cash is short.)
- Don't, under any circumstances, spend or commit any money on a project until you have it in the bank. The

charity world is littered with the debris of initiatives that have been cancelled or reduced because a fundraising event was rained off, a marathon runner fell down a rabbit hole in training and couldn't raise his £2,000; or, more seriously, a trust or major donor didn't come through with a grant to fund an important project, or a corporate supporter ran into unexpected financial difficulties. Wait until the money promised is banked and the cheque cleared. Then spend it!

- Focus. What are you trying to do? It is very common to have too much to do, too many opportunities and to get distracted from the main purpose of the venture. Following the funding is seductive. Several times in the history of Whizz-Kidz, people have had bright ideas for other work the charity could do; from opening international offices to helping young adults over the age of eighteen become mobile. All well-intentioned and valuable, but the charity was formed to help provide mobility equipment for disabled children in Britain under the age of eighteen. So far we have helped about 5,000, and we estimate that there are 70,000 who need such equipment. So let's get that cracked before we diversify. The most important thing is to keep the most important thing the most important thing!

- Regularly ask yourself the simple question: 'Are we doing the best we can for the people we are trying to help?' The answer to this question is always no. But it does help to keep everyone concentrating on trying to do the best they possibly can for those they are trying to help. It is real customer service.

- Fuss the staff and the volunteers. They are the charity. I know this is what they say in business, but it's different.

Choose intelligent, enthusiastic people, involve them in the cause and the decision-making process, and they will take on the world. Prepare to be argued with lots. If you have done your job properly these people will be bright and care. That is good news.

- There will always be more 'need' than you can cope with. Settle down to make real progress in each area of work, each year. Evolution not revolution.
- Involve the people you help. Find regular and informal ways of talking to and communicating with the people you are trying to support. The Kidz Board at Whizz-Kidz is one of the most powerful initiatives that we ever began. The presence of the children hugely motivated the staff and the fundraisers. Ask those in this group to trustee meetings. Be wary of establishing a users' council unless you are prepared to delay taking important decisions while consultations take place. Be well placed to consult but never abdicate executive authority.
- Always involve and speak to the people doing the front-line work. Remember that potential funders would much rather meet these people than the fundraising team and sometimes even you! They want to talk to the people who are going to use their money.
- Anyone who can or will raise money for your charity is a gem and should be hugged regularly. Customer care also applies to those who provide your income, and sadly the charity world is not alone in neglecting to thank its donors properly and keep them in touch with the charity's work. Some people in charities even regard fundraisers as a necessary evil! If you don't have any income you can't do any useful work. The End!

Chapter 5

PHILANTHROPY

'philanthropy n. 1 a love of humankind. 2 practical benevolence, esp. charity on a large scale.'

Oxford Dictionary

'...yet the day is not too far distant when the man who dies leaving millions of available wealth, which was free to him to administer during life, will pass away "unwept, unhonored, and unsung", no matter to what uses he leaves the dross which he cannot take with him. Of such as these the public verdict will then be: "The man who dies thus rich dies disgraced."'

Andrew Carnegie

Is there really a rise in philanthropy in the UK? Is it contributing significant new money to the charity sector? Is it even becoming fashionable?

We read of the enormous generosity of Bill and Melinda Gates, and, nearer to home, Anita Roddick, J.K. Rowling, Lord David Sainsbury and Sir Tom Hunter. Surely the answer is yes?

Well, the facts tell a different story.

Charitable donations from the public (including long-established trusts and legacies) have been static over the past decade. As a percentage of overall income, the trend is steadily declining.

Over the same period the wealth of the richest 1,000 people in the land has more than trebled (according to the *Sunday Times* Rich List), and the UK's wealth management industry – stockbrokers, private banks and the like – are enjoying a boom. Assets managed were up by 22 per cent in 2006. And that doesn't include the 100,000 new people who began managing their money directly online in the same year. The same survey estimates that those with liquid assets of over £144,000 now number 2.35 million and their wealth totals £1,433,000 (UK Wealth Management Industry Report 2007: ComPeer Ltd). Different research (where the definition of mass affluent requires you to have over £200,000 in liquid assets) show numbers increasing by 27 per cent between 2003 and 2005 to 877,000, while these assets grew faster by 32 per cent to £541 billion (UK High Net Worth Customers 2006: Datamonitor).

Projections confidently predict further growth. 'Sustained explosion of wealth' is a phrase used by those who earn a living researching the area. By 2010 1.34 million of us will have liquid assets of £847 billion. The greatest proportion will have between £2 million and £5 million of LIQUID assets – i.e. not counting your house.

How people give has also been researched. A fraction under 70 per cent of these people currently make charitable donations of up to £500 a year (Euromonitor), and very nearly as many (67 per cent) would leave money to their family rather than to charity. Not all following Andrew Carnegie, then.

So is there really a rise in individual philanthropy? My answer must be: a little. People are becoming more aware, with a few seriously committed and some setting a great example. But we're a long way away from the tipping point. Where generosity of spirit is acknowledged as something to take pride in which will contribute more to your individual happiness than conspicuous consumption or making a killing in the investment market. Where one definition of a millionaire might be a person who 'gives' a million away.

Which brings me nicely to bonuses. The Office of National Statistics recorded UK bonus payments of £26 billion in the period December 2006 to April 2007. Of this, £14 billion was paid to those working in the financial sector, mainly in the City of London. Interestingly, the remaining £12 billion was paid in other sectors including manufacturing, retailing and the public sector.

It is worth pausing to reflect on these extraordinary figures and to grasp that these are *bonuses* – i.e. remuneration paid *on top* of the people's salaries.

And this is a recurring amount, certainly in the City. In other words, it is fresh money earned every year. This differentiates it in the main from wealth created elsewhere throughout the UK, which is mostly based on building businesses up and selling them. Or, inevitably, the increase in property values.

BONUS TIME!

If you are lucky enough to be someone who receives a bonus – well done. You probably deserve it, either because you have sacrificed much of your spare time, worked long hours, allowed family relationships to slip, been stressed and even seen your health suffer. It is not my place to comment on any of this, about how you should live your life, or the right and wrongs of the size of your bonus. And anyway, I couldn't begin to grasp the complexities of private equity, hedge funds and the rest.

But I would like you to take some time out to think through some of the issues raised in this book. What *is* enough for you and your family? (See page 28.) How are you going to make the transformation from 'Success to Significance'? (See page 25.) Given that you have been able to earn this money in a free country, do you not think you should give some time and a proportion of your new wealth to help more disadvantaged people? In short, could you become a friend of the weak? Martin Luther King Jr summed it up well: 'Life's most persistent and urgent question is: What are you doing for others?'

Email me and I will show you how to give effectively, and who to give it to:

mikedickson@themoreyougive.co.uk

It is reasonably clear to everyone in Britain that there is a widening gap between rich and poor. And indeed now between the very rich and the increasingly stretched middle classes.

The *Sunday Times* Rich List published a Giving Index in 2007, claiming a big increase in charitable giving by the top thirty donors, who gave £1.2 billion in 2006, up from £453 million the previous year. Hooray! Well, sort of. Actually, nearly a half of this increased sum was made up from two gifts: one of £511 million by mining magnate Anil Agarwal to build a university in India; and another of £100.3 million given by David and Heather Stevens, two of the founders of Admiral Insurance, to start the Waterloo Foundation, which hopes to be able to distribute about £4 million a year to a range of causes including 'the developing world, the environment, children's development and the local community in South Wales where Admiral is based'.

Take those amounts from the 2005 figure and you get an increase of £148 million. Not exactly a philanthropic boom!

So what is going to be done about all this? I would like to argue that we can all do our part. Happiness doesn't rise exponentially the more we have. So, if you want to be happy, and are lucky enough not to need everything you earn to feed, house and clothe your family, try giving. Before stashing it away, buying more stuff, or investing it for your old age – give some away. You can afford it.

Philanthropy Advisers

At the moment, the new breed of 'philanthropy advisers', those who act as a conduit for funds between the large-scale givers and the charities – of which I am one – do not contribute much when put against the total levels of charity giving.

Total charitable donations by the public, companies, trusts (including legacies) in 2006–7 amounted to about £13 billion. Against this sum, the philanthropy advisers' contribution is very small. It is not that everyone doesn't mean well and try hard. It is just that it is a very small sum overall.

New Philanthropy Capital claims to be enabling £1 million per month to be given to charities; Impetus Trust has distributed £8 million over four years and is raising

PHILANTHROPY

another fund of £30 million to spend. The Institute of Philanthropy has no figures, and Philanthropy UK provides general advice and support, but does not advise on specific donations.

ARK, the hedge fund charity, raised £26.6 million at their annual gala. (Yes, you did read that correctly: £26.6 million in one night.) Even so, if you add it all up and multiply it by two it might equal £100 million a year maximum – a drop in the pond of the £41 billion annual income to charities.

Compare this with the money given by the major grant-making trusts, such as Henry Smith, Garfield Weston, the various Sainsbury Trusts and many others, which amounts to £3 billion a year. And they have been distributing these sorts of sums for a long time.

There are two ways of responding to this sad and unequal state of affairs. You could get very cross – especially if you are amongst the poorer sections of society – or you can try to make the case for a more enlightened and generous approach, and find heroes of good heart to set forward as examples of how to behave.

Which is the route I prefer to take. People like Sir Tom Hunter, Stanley Fink, Sir Peter Lampl, Dr Frederick Mulder, Christopher Hohn and others have begun to give very large amounts, sensibly, sensitively and systematically. These are people who have been successful in one area of life and now have the time, the resources and the contacts to bring to charities and causes which excite, inspire or (in many cases) anger them. And the will to make a difference. They want to be involved and they look for the impact that their donation or investment will have.

Some of these people use city language and still bang on

about 'ROI' and leverage. Try as I might, I cannot spend much time discussing this without losing consciousness. ('You are supposed to be motivated by helping PEOPLE!' I want to say.) But for the most part, this whole approach, of looking to see how money can be used to improve the performance of a charity, and therefore increase its impact and ability to help, is extremely positive. And they do have a point. Until very recently most charities were not known for their management skills. Very few had any idea of what success actually looked like; many still don't. When a CEO of a charity is asked by an intelligent, wealthy person: 'If I give you this money, what difference will it make?' it is a seminal moment. Not like 'the good old days' when wealthy individuals gave the charity a cheque and politely left them to use it as they saw fit. And unlike Victorian philanthropy, which generally assumed 'superior wisdom', today's philanthropists take pains to research and talk to the real experts – those working at the coal face.

My take on all this is positive. The donors become more involved in the charity and the cause, not least because they derive personal satisfaction from being involved – from feeling part of something useful and worthwhile and mixing with people in the charity world who initially seem to them to be from another star system but in fact show themselves to be inspired, driven and passionate.

The majority of the people I meet who have 'done well', or had what private banks rather quaintly call 'a liquidity event', are always interesting sometimes fascinating people who have made a mark. By the same token, people who have started a charity, or indeed lead one, are usually inspirational people who care passionately about what they do. Introducing one to the other can be hugely uplifting.

It is an interesting thought that most of the UK's leading philanthropists began life in relatively modest backgrounds. It is almost as if those who have been poor and then made money, 'get it'. They go back to their roots, remember their upbringing and give to the poorest section of society in Britain (and increasingly the world) with more 'sympathico'. It is certainly true that, with a few honourable exceptions, those with inherited wealth give less.

It is also true that many high earners and wealthy people in the City and the UK simply do *not* get it. They are still hoarding, buying toys and showing off at deeply embarrassing charity auctions.

US Philanthropy

Americans are almost twice as generous as the British (although it was British Victorian philanthropy which inspired American philanthropy).

Giving USA estimates that Americans (both individual and corporate) gave total contributions of $260.28 billion in 2004–5, a growth of 6.1 per cent and mostly due to unprecedented giving to domestic and foreign disasters. Individual giving is always the largest single source of donations in America. This rose by 6.4 percent (2.9 percent adjusted for inflation) to an estimated $199.07 billion. This accounts for 76.5 per cent of all estimated giving in 2004–5 and represents 1.75 per cent of GDP.

Using the same measure for the same year, UK individual giving was £8.9 billion, 0.76 per cent of GDP. Less than half.

> In America, planned giving accounts for 61 per cent of income to charities; whereas in the UK over 60 per cent of income to charities is 'spontaneous'.
>
> In the USA, 35 per cent of employees give to charity through their payroll; a pitiful 2 per cent of UK employees give this way.

Americans are used to giving. Success is celebrated, and when they achieve success they become generous donors. Especially to their communities, churches, educational establishments and universities, and to art galleries, orchestras and museums.

There is a social cachet to 'giving something back'. Personal benefit, in the form of peer approval, improved social status and involvement are accepted. Americans are sceptical of government bureaucracy, and would rather spend their own money on their favourite causes, taking full advantage of the tax breaks. They generally believe that they are better managers of these institutions than their government, whereas the British, perhaps because of government-funded health and education systems, seem to think that the State should pay for most things, whilst keeping our taxes as low as possible. A very questionable equation.

American universities, for example, have excellent and powerful alumni programmes, which continuously tap into their graduates, who in turn feel a responsibility to support their old universities as 'repayment' for their education. In the UK, alumni programmes are much less developed and there is little sense of 'owing' for what is still, by any standards, an excellent, almost free education.

American Philanthropists Old and New

In America, these two examples of large-scale philanthropy – Andrew Carnegie and Bill Gates – show how far ahead the USA is in terms of giving, both historically and in modern life.

Andrew Carnegie

The Scottish-born philanthropist was famously 'the richest man in the world' in the early twentieth century. Carnegie went to America with his family when he was thirteen and started work as a bobbin boy in a cotton mill, followed by a series of other jobs. In 1865 he started the Carnegie Steel company, which he eventually sold to the bank JP Morgan for $480 million.

His famous essay, 'The Gospel of Wealth', written in 1889, is required reading for anyone who has done well, and a free copy should be mandatory with every bonus cheque at the end of the year. He devoted the rest of his life to philanthropy and gave away most of his wealth, more than $350 million. Amongst other things, he built 2,509 libraries throughout America and the world. The Carnegie Corporation of New York was created to enable 'the advancement and diffusion of knowledge and understanding'. The grants were to be used 'for the benefit of the people of the United States, although up to 7.5 per cent could be used for the same purpose in countries that have been or are members of the British Commonwealth' with a current emphasis on Africa.

Carnegie didn't believe that a wealthy man should leave his money to his children, and certainly not the State. It should be given away in his own lifetime for the good of others in the community. This is what he wrote:

> This then, is held to be the duty of the man of wealth: to set an example of modest, unostentatious living, shunning display or extravagance; to provide moderately for the legitimate wants of those dependent on him; and, after doing so, to consider all surplus revenues which come upon him simply as trust funds, which he is called upon to administer, and strictly bound as a matter of duty to administer in the manner which, in his judgement, is best calculated to produce the most beneficial results for the community – the man of wealth thus becoming the mere trustee and agent for his poorer brethren, bringing to their service his superior wisdom, experience and ability to administer, doing better than they would or could do for themselves.

In 2006, The Carnegie Corporation's capital fund, originally donated at a value of about $135 million, had a market value of approximately $2.5 billion. In 2007 it expects to make grants totalling approximately $90 million.

Bill and Melinda Gates – 'Billanthropy'

The Bill and Melinda Gates Foundation is philanthropy on such a huge scale that it is sometimes difficult to grasp. Maybe it is the donations worth billions, rather than mere millions. Or the impact that the Foundation has in 'setting an example'. Warren Buffet's decision to give 10,000

Berkshire Hathaway shares worth $30.7 million to the Foundation rather than start his own, effectively doubled its annual giving programme.

Bill Gates founded Microsoft in 1975, famously to put 'a computer on every desk and in every home'. He is now the world's second richest man with an estimated net worth of $56 billion and chairs The Bill and Melinda Gates Foundation, which controls an astonishing endowment of $33.4 billion and concentrates its focus on AIDS, and finding a vaccine for malaria and hepatitis B. Since its inception the Foundation has given grants totalling $13.6 billion ($1.56 billion in 2006 alone). Nearly $8 billion has gone into their global health programme including $1.8 billion into HIV, TB and reproductive health. The Foundation's global development programme helps some of the world poorest people, especially farmers, to improve crop production and market access, and, through organisations such as the Grameen Bank, to access financial services and microloans that could lift them out of poverty by building small businesses and accumulating some assets of their own.

Gates has said that his children will not inherit enormous wealth.

UK Philanthropy

In Britain just 5 per cent of the population – those that make regular gifts of more than £50 per month (£600 per year) – provide over half of all voluntary income to charities. The anomaly is that the wealthiest fifth of the population only give about 1 per cent of their earnings, whilst the poorest fifth in our society give on average just under 3 per cent.

If you pause to think about it for a moment, it means that a person earning £50,000 gives away just £500 a year, and that someone earning £100,000 gives away £1,000 a year. It puts a whole new meaning into disposable income.

By and large, wealthy individuals in Britain make their money and head for the hills. It is still perceived as 'not the done thing' to display your wealth or your generosity, in complete contrast to those who make money in America. This modest behaviour would normally be praiseworthy but for two factors.

The first is that it masks a true lack of generosity, or at the very least an unwillingness to take the subject of philanthropy seriously and thoughtfully, to think about the problems faced by the less fortunate members of society and act decently to help them. Some do respond to an appeal from a good cause by writing a cheque, others have 'sleeping' accounts with Charities Aid Foundation, and many do have interests in certain causes, which they support on a semi-regular basis. And of course there are those who still continue to pay daft sums for charity auction prizes, the 'signed England Rugby Shirt' syndrome, almost always the other end of copious amounts of red wine or egged on by their friends.

There are some wonderfully enlightened individuals, who have grasped the plot, realise how fortunate they are, and set off to use their tremendous wealth and influence for the good of others. But there are not that many. And even they tend to do it quietly. Secondly, a modest approach does little to set an example to your family, children, friends or other people you know who could give much more but don't. Or to other members of the public.

It is these two things, the miserly behaviour of some

wealthy people, coupled with the genuine modesty of those who are extremely generous, that holds back levels of giving by high net worth individuals in this country, and drives some in the charity sector to drink. As Oscar Wilde said: 'There is only one class in the community that thinks more about money than the rich, and that is the poor.'

Fortunately things are starting to change. There is a new group of British philanthropists who, though small in number, are beginning to set an example.

The New UK Philanthropists

Sir Tom Hunter

This Scottish financier started life as the son of a modest family grocer and watched the coal mining village he lived in plunged into poverty when Scotland's state-supported mining industry collapsed in the late eighties. He went on to build a successful chain of sports shops, which he sold at the age of thirty-seven for £260 million. He created the Hunter Foundation with his wife Marion in 1998 because it was tax efficient, 'without knowing very much about it' and with an initial donation of £10 million, later giving £100 million to the foundation from his personal fortune to 'support the development of a more enterprising and ultimately more entrepreneurial society in Scotland' principally invested in enterprise and educational initiatives aimed at children. He has since made significant donations to Band Aid, the Make Poverty History campaign and the tsunami appeal, and teamed up with Bill Clinton with a donation of $100 million to a joint development initiative in Malawi and Rwanda. This year he announced his intention to give £1 billion to charity, though interestingly this aim is couched in unusual terms: 'The aim is to redouble our efforts in wealth creation through West Coast Capital [a private equity partnership] in order that we can, over time, invest £1 billion in venture philanthropy through our foundation. Great wealth brings with it great responsibility.' So it is not a donation from his current wealth, rather an interesting commitment to use his talent to make further money for the purpose of charity.

Sir Elton John

The rock star gave £22.4 million in 2006 to The Elton John AIDS Foundation (EJAF), a UK-registered charity that exists to empower people infected, affected and at risk of HIV/AIDS: 'To alleviate their physical, emotional and financial hardship, enabling them to improve their quality of life, live with dignity and exercise self-determination.' The charity was established in 1993 by Sir Elton John. A sister organisation with an office in Los Angeles was established in 1992 to fund programmes in North America. It works with other organisations such as the Clinton Foundation.

In the past fourteen years the two organisations have raised over $110 million and supported over four thousand projects in fifty-five countries worldwide. More than 12 million people have been assisted. The foundation is the largest independent funder of HIV/AIDS projects within the United Kingdom. During 2005, it awarded grants totalling over £1 million to support thirty-nine UK projects and is currently supporting 128 projects in seventeen countries.

Peter Cruddas

According to the *Sunday Times* Rich List in 2007, Cruddas is the City's richest man, worth over £1 billion. He recently announced plans to give £100 million through his foundation to a variety of causes including The Duke of Edinburgh award scheme, Great Ormond Street Hospital and the Prince's Trust. The Cruddas fortune was built by starting CMC Markets in 1989, now considered a global leader in online financial trading.

Like many philanthropists, Peter came from humble beginnings. His father was a Smithfield meat-market porter, his mother a cleaner, and he left Shoreditch Comprehensive in the East End of London at sixteen to help support a family that included his cab-driving twin brother. 'I think it is quite obscene for one person to have such a large amount of money,' he has said. Quite right.

Christopher Hohn

This 39-year-old graduate of Southampton University and son of a white Jamaican car mechanic who emigrated to Britain in 1960, is known for being both 'an aggressive investor', and extremely shy. He doesn't comment on his charitable giving, and his American wife Jamie is also deeply reluctant to discuss their philanthropy: 'We are just not really interested in putting more information out there' Christopher channels a significant amount of the profits from his Children's Investment Fund – one of the most successful hedge funds in Europe – into his charitable foundation, which works to alleviate child poverty in the developing world and is run by Jamie. It is said to take a very business-like approach to the projects it backs, looking for proof of positive benefits for the children it tries to help, and projects that can be 'scaled up' to help thousands.

Christopher, who was a Baker Scholar at Harvard Business School and cut his trading teeth on Wall Street, went it alone in 2003, and set up the charity link in order 'to motivate his own performance'.

In 2005 he emerged as Britain's most generous philanthropist, giving away more than £50 million to children's charities in the developing world. In 2006 the Children's Investment Fund made a huge donation of £230 million to his charitable foundation.

The Sainsbury Family

Lord David Sainsbury sees his family's history of giving as the main reason he established the Gatsby Charitable Foundation in 1967. He'd inherited a substantial shareholding at the age of twenty-seven and it seemed natural to give some of it away.

The foundation was small and carried his personal stamp. Today it still supports causes he believes in, takes risks and is prepared to work towards long-term results.

In 1993 he made the largest recorded personal donation to his trust: £300 million. The foundation is one of nineteen Sainsbury Family Trusts set up by different family members sharing common administration and knowledge. It has given away more than £400 million over the past thirty-five years and has £100 million already committed to charities and projects in the future. In May 2005, Lord Sainsbury announced that he intended to become the first Briton to give away at least £1 billion in his lifetime (now joined by Scottish businessman Tom Hunter) and that he would be instructing his foundation to spend both capital and interest so that it would be wound up after his death.

His rationale is that donors who spend their own money are more likely to innovate and take risks than trustees. He is committed to change, knows this takes time, and is encouraged by the work that can make an amazing difference for relatively small sums. For example, he cites research which developed a disease-resistant strain of cassava, a staple crop that used to be devastated, like clockwork, every three years. Now the yields are higher every year and, in Lord Sainsbury's words, 'It's difficult to conceive of any project that I've done which has had more impact in terms of improving the quality of people's lives.' With a hands-on approach, he says, 'you begin to know where the good people are' and can support them.

The family tradition is being continued. Each of Lord Sainsbury's three daughters has their own foundation and has picked areas of interest: 'It means they have the same kind of fun and involvement that I've had.'

The New Philanthropists – Profiles

STANLEY FINK

This story says a lot about our next philanthropist.

Stanley Fink won a scholarship to a grammar school in Manchester. When he had become a wealthy man he was approached by the headmaster of his old school and asked if he would donate to the school's scholarship fund, with his name heading the fund.

Stanley decided that he would prefer to pay money for the whole education of one child, and to make the financial contribution anonymously. His only request was that the pupil should receive an unsigned letter when finishing at the school which read: 'Your education has been paid for by old boy of the school who got his education free and has done rather well in life. He decided that this was a good way to give something back, so if you ever find yourself in such a fortunate position, think about it.'

It was the first of many scholarships he funded at this and other schools.

Stanley Fink speaks very quietly. And he gives quietly. And thoughtfully. More impressively, he has been giving all his life, not just since becoming a wealthy man. A 'generosity of spirit' is very much a part of his DNA.

When I was talking to people about Stanley, someone who knows him well called him a 'prince amongst men'. Slightly less effusively, another described him as 'a role model for modern philanthropy'. He would be embarrassed by this sort of remark – but he really is rather special. This is a man whose achievements include, in no particular order: starting out from a modest background to become one of the wealthiest men in Britain; being happily married for twenty-six years; helping to develop ARK, the hedge fund charity and to raising £10 million for the new Evelina children's hospital; donating a significant sum to, and becoming chairman of, a new Academy school in West London; surviving a brain tumour in his early forties. And that is without mentioning numerous private acts of generosity.

Stanley's parents tithed, which Stanley – a liberal Jew – thinks is one of the positive attributes that the faiths have in common. He started his own charitable work at the age

PHILANTHROPY

of eighteen in Manchester, giving time rather than money – 'I didn't have much money' – and later joined the Round Table. He discovered that the people he met doing charitable work were generally outgoing and generous-spirited, and that 'most people can give, money or time – some are fortunate enough to give both, that is fantastic, but very few people have the excuse not to do either.'

Giving was harder when he was building a career, grappling with a mortgage and starting a family. He joined Man Group at the age of twenty-nine and when the company was floated on the stock exchange in 1994 he suddenly had cash, and began to develop his own philosophy about giving.

He treated himself to the 'toys' that come with wealth, but also always continued to look for ways of quietly helping a member of his family or friends who were experiencing difficult times, as well as charitable causes. He believes that true philanthropy is a mixture of giving to registered charities and helping the people around you, but believes that 'the highest order of philanthropy is to try and do it anonymously.'

Education remains his real passion and he believes in the saying: 'Give a man a fish and feed him for a day, but teach a man to fish and feed him for life.' His other interests include basic healthcare, especially for children, and social welfare, including humane treatment of the elderly and other disadvantaged groups in society. He is currently looking at environmental causes.

When he is giving he looks for:

- An individual with passion, and the competence to get the job done: 'Quite a good idea implemented really well can be magical – but a great idea badly implemented

will result in nothing. Implementation is as important as the inspiration. If you can find both then that's great.'
- The cause itself: 'Is teaching children to read more important than teaching children to appreciate art?' For him it is a rhetorical question.
- How many bangs do you get for your buck? 'Can the funds be used to finish a project, for example? How many children can you educate for a million pounds?'

STANLEY FINK ON PHILANTHROPY

If you are fortunate enough to be rich there are some key questions you need to ask yourself:

- **How much do you expect to earn by the end of your life?**
- **How much do you expect to spend on yourself for the rest of your life?**
- **How much do you think it is right to leave to your children?**
- **What do you expect to do with the balance?**
- **What do you ultimately want to achieve with your good fortune?**
- **Do you want to die the richest man in the graveyard? There is a good Jewish expression: Better to give with a warm hand, than with a cold hand!**

To end on another story: When one of Stanley's sons had his bar mitzvah – when traditionally the child comes of age and receives lots of presents – their son offered to give 20 per cent of his cash presents to charity. He chose a local school run by the RNIB (The Royal National Institute for the Blind), visited the charity with his mother and handed over his cheque. A well-centred son, a very proud father, and proof that setting an example is as important as preaching generosity.

SIR PETER LAMPL

Sir Peter's involvement in philanthropy began after he anonymously funded the campaign to ban the ownership of handguns, following the massacre of children in Dunblane, Scotland. Having lived in America, Peter 'felt strongly that handguns were not a good idea', and a meeting in his living room with the father of one of the victims spurred him to act. When the British Government changed in May 1997, new legislation was proposed to declare all hand-guns illegal. This measure became law in November 1997. It was his first realisation that one individual could really make a difference.

Shortly afterwards he went back to see his old school in Reigate, which had been a free grammar school. Now it is a fee-paying independent school. He realised that he and many of his schoolfriends wouldn't have been able to go there now. The situation came into sharper focus when he visited his old college at Oxford, and discovered that less than half of the students came from state schools. In his days, the figure had been two-thirds. It was, as he saw it, a form of 'social apartheid'.

'We live in a very unfair country,' he says. 'I get up every morning feeling outraged at how we treat kids so badly. It is hugely unfair that young people from certain backgrounds don't have the opportunities that are commensurate with their ability; they get a lousy deal. It is something I feel very strongly about. I can't think of a better way to spend my time and money than trying to do something about it ... I am always coming across well-to-do people who say that their children can't get into Oxford and Cambridge even though they have four A-levels and isn't it impossible ... There is an expectation amongst many people that if you come from a certain class, have spent the money on private education, you're entitled to get an Oxbridge place ...'

Social mobility is defined as 'the ability of people to change their social position within the society.' In practical terms this means the ability of people from a poorer background to move up the social and economic ladder. Britain has the lowest social mobility of any advanced nation for which figures are available. Research commissioned by the Sutton Trust shows that social mobility in Britain has declined for those born in the 1970s compared to those born in the 1950s – in other words, it has become tougher, not easier, for those at the bottom to get to the top. And even though the absolute number of university places has grown, this expansion has overwhelmingly benefited the middle classes.

In 1997 Sir Peter set up the Sutton Trust to provide educational opportunities for able young people from non-privileged backgrounds. He started by persuading Oxford University to begin a week-long summer school for state school students who came from families with no experience of university, to raise their aspirations and encourage them to apply.

Only ten years later, almost 1,000 Year 12 students (those who come from non-professional backgrounds, are the first in their family to study at university, and who attend state schools with low higher education progression rates) take part in the Sutton Trust Summer Schools every year, gaining the opportunity to sample university life and teaching, to meet undergraduates and to gain a better understanding of the application process. Since the first summer school at Oxford University, the project has expanded to Bristol, Cambridge, Nottingham, St Andrews and, in a modified form, to a number of other universities. The summer schools will run for the eleventh year in 2007. The Government has picked up this model and now funds summer schools (for Year 11 students) at the majority of British universities.

As Sir Peter points out, if ten students in 100 attending the summer schools change their life course and go onto an elite research university the impact of the Sutton Trust is significant. The value to a young person of a degree from an elite research university over a post-92 university is on average around £80,000.

Of course they also receive an excellent education in the subject that they have chosen to study. But there are many non-financial benefits to going to university, both individually and for society – graduates are more likely to vote, to enjoy a healthy diet and lifestyle, to give blood, to participate in their community.

It is social mobility in action.

It would be interesting to measure the impact of the Sutton Trust on individual lives. How many young people have had their lives transformed by the vision and determination of one man? And what are they all doing now?

→ www.suttontrust.com

THE MORE YOU GIVE, THE MORE YOU GET

DAVID ROBINSON

David Robinson is a remarkable man. The founder of **Community Links**, and the inspiration for **We Are What We Do**, David is a quiet-mannered, sensible, well-informed person committed to helping people. He inspires literally thousands of people to 'take action' in a variety of extraordinary ways, possibly because under his quiet exterior there lurks a 'can do' attitude coupled with a hint of mischief! David established Community Links over thirty years ago and it has now come to be recognised as an outstanding model of a community-based charity. Eighty per cent of their staff were previously clients, and over 100 different languages are spoken across their services. In 2005–6 over 50,000 lives were touched by their projects in Newham and the East End of London: from visiting elderly and isolated people and helping them claim benefits to the value of £746,000, to placing long-term unemployed young people into sustainable jobs, to helping people for whom English may be their second or even third language and who may have literacy problems, to running education programmes for young people who have been excluded from school and often have complex family problems.

In 2012, the Olympic Games will take place in the East End. It will only account for 20 per cent of the money being spent on regenerating the area, but it presents a unique 'once in a lifetime' opportunity to transform the area physically. But what of the communities living there? What will be their future? What will happen to the social environment? For David Robinson this is *the* core issue. Will the excluded communities that Community Links helps simply be moved somewhere else, where they will remain poor and excluded, or involved and integrated in to the new development? He points to the example of Canary Wharf, which is a huge success in financial terms but has become an island of wealth. The development didn't regenerate local communities, rather 'moved them further down the A13'.

David uses a simple analogy to describe the task ahead for Community Links. The charity can either 'continue to run the ambulance at the bottom of the cliff helping relatively small numbers of people, or they can put their efforts into building fences at the top of the cliff in the hope that one day they won't need the ambulance'.

COMMUNITY LINKS MISSION STATEMENT

'To generate change. To tackle causes not symptoms; find solutions not palliatives. To recognise that we all need to give as well as to receive, and to appreciate that those who experience a problem understand it best. To act local but to think global; teach but never stop learning. To distinguish between the diversity that enriches our society and the inequalities that diminish it. To grow but all to build a network not an empire. To be driven by dreams and judged on delivery. To never do things for people but to guide and support, to train and enable, to simply inspire.'

DR FREDERICK MULDER ('FRED')

I first met Fred the day after he had won an award for creative philanthropy at the annual Beacon Awards. A quiet and rather diffident Canadian, Fred is a highly respected and successful print dealer. He is also an inspiration to many givers, and a wonderfully generous and creative philanthropist. (His only weakness is his passionate support for Arsenal!)

When Greenpeace's boat, *Rainbow Warrior*, was blown up in Auckland harbour in 1985, Fred approached Greenpeace, then a comparatively young organisation, with an idea. He would underwrite the cost of advertisements on the front pages of newspapers, where news of the sinking of the *Rainbow Warrior* was appearing daily, to attract new members and donations. The ads were extremely successful, donations poured in and membership increased enormously.

In one of those 'a-ha' moments, Fred told me that one of the best things a funder can do for a charity is 'to take a risk that the organisation can't afford to take'. A good clue to his entrepreneurial approach to philanthropy.

Another inventive application to giving involved a dispute with his neighbours over access to a piece of his land. After each neighbour had got legal advice and presumably commensurate bills, there was deadlock. Fred's solution was inspired. He realised that the land had a value to his neighbours, and felt that there should be some cost, but he didn't need to be the financial beneficiary. So he suggested that they should all have equal access to the land, and he offered to put £25,000 into a pot if the others would do the same. The money, £125,000 in total, would be given to fund an educational project in Zambia administered by Oxfam. The dispute was quickly ended, and the shared enterprise created real benefits. One of which was his feelings about his neighbours, who became friends, colleagues and partners, rather than foes.

With a glint of mischief in his eye he tells of another 'quirky' act of philanthropy. An American professor wanted to buy two prints from Fred's private collection that he didn't want to sell. At all. After a little agonising Fred offered to give him the prints free – but there was a catch. He asked the professor to give away the *value* of the prints. The slightly bemused professor agreed, and together they decided to give the money to an Indian hospital performing cataract operations. (The professor had just had a cataract operation!) I asked Fred about the psychology of this. After all, if he didn't want to sell the prints *and* he got no money for them – well, it just seemed strange to say the least. He paused. 'Well, I realised that although I did really want to keep those prints, I wanted something else more, and the desire to achieve this "something else" trumped the desire to keep those prints.'

Fred's personal approach to philanthropy is split in two: the first issue is finding causes that appeal to him – international development, microfinance, the environment, economic justice and conflict prevention; the second is entrepreneurship and risk, which probably influences him more. He tends to give when the two intersect. He loves organisations and people that have a buzz, but importantly that have to have the capacity to get something done. As he says, there are lots of people with great ideas to improve the world but have no idea of how to go about doing it.

Why does giving play such an important part in Fred's life?

'Everybody wants to make a positive difference in the world ... If you are fortunate enough to have the financial wherewithal, it is a wonderful thing to be able to do. Making someone happy, comfortable, feel loved or accepted or safe is a very powerful thing . . . There are certain things that you want to see done in giving terms that are about your own values and the values your would like to see embedded in the world. You can't do it because you don't have the skills, are too busy doing something else or don't have the time. Then you find wonderful people who ARE doing it and you think, "Oh my God" that needs to be done, but I can't do it, I'll help those people to do it – that's a much better way.'

Would that more people were so generous and imaginative with their giving.

Fred is also one of the founders and chair of The Funding Network (see page 82).

DAVID GOLD

David Gold is enthusiastic, energetic – in a Duracell sort of way – positive and very good company. His approach to philanthropy is based on 'trust and risk'. Taking risks on people and trusting them to deliver. It is a sharp contrast to some of the current 'noise' about philanthropy in the City, which talks about 'leverage' and 'return on investment' to decide on their involvement in charity. In 2001 David started the UK office of A Glimmer of Hope, a private foundation established in America by his sister and brother-in-law. The Trust is an independent funder, which allows it to take calculated risks, and uses its own network of contacts to find innovative projects, led by good people who have trouble finding funding.

The trust focuses its work on building the self-esteem and skills of excluded youth under the age of twenty-five through equality of opportunity and respect. David describes this as 'the operating software for getting on in life'. He loves the enthusiasm of young people and hates to see them being written off so early in their lives due to lack of opportunity. And he also feels strongly that the majority of current grant-making is inherently conservative and undervalues knowledge and intuition. A large part of his analysis is: 'Would I trust this person over a period of time? Have they got passion and compassion?' So he does something original with the people and organisations he funds: he talks to them, keeps in regular contact and remains an engaged investor. He writes the cheque, then stays in touch, but doesn't demand written reports: 'If I can get on my scooter and be somewhere in half an hour and spend forty-five minutes with them, that's a much shorter time than it would probably take to read and comment on a report. More importantly a much, much shorter time than it would take them to write it.'

A Glimmer of Hope has successfully funded:

Shpresa – which means hope in Albanian – set up in 2000 by a remarkable woman called Luljeta Nuzi, to enable Albanian-speaking refugees, asylum-seekers and migrants to settle in the UK, gain confidence, make progress in their life and participate in society.

Luljeta has achieved remarkable results. Shpresa now has four full-time staff, thirty-one volunteers, five sessional staff, 900 paid members and over 2000 users. Every week the charity helps more than 350 people.

From working just in Newham, Shpresa has expanded its services to other boroughs such as Barking, Redbridge, Islington and Haringey. One of its young people is representing the charity at the Youth Parliament, it has won the Queen's award and been to Buckingham Palace garden parties, and has taken part in discussions about the voluntary sector at 10 Downing Street.

Luljeta says: 'A Glimmer of Hope trusted us when we had nothing else apart from the passion for our work, a clear need for the project to happen and maybe not enough experience of running the project. Their funding supported us to prove that this project could have a real impact on people's life, and give us the opportunity to try things and be as creative as we could. David for me is a very inspiring person, I admire the way he works, he is simple and he has got excellent communication skills. Someone who knows to value your skills and doesn't put you down because of your background or your level of English etc. He is very understanding and builds up your hopes and dreams. He has an excellent team who he works with, and who have been great support to us as well.

'A Glimmer of Hope was a glimmer of hope for us and I am pretty sure that without their support we might not have been as successful as we are today.'

A Glimmer of Hope has provided funding to the tune of £90,000.

→ www.shpresaprogramme.com

DAVID GOLD ON PHILANTHROPY

1. **If it feels good, do it.**
2. **Seek to enjoy it. This is really important.**
3. **Open yourself to engage with people.**
4. **Invest in issues you feel passionate about.**
5. **Be patient. Stick with it despite the odd setback.**

PHILANTHROPY

> 6. Ask 'open' questions.
> 7. Visit charities. It costs very little to hop on a bike. Even get a cab. You will always be bowled over by how enthusiastic they are to see you. I can't think of a better way of getting engaged.
> 8. Take a risk with people.

At the end of the interview, I ask David what he thinks are the rewards of giving.

For a while he is quiet, and still – itself unusual. Then he is off: 'It is great to play a part in a charity's success – you feel part of their family, part of society if you are genuinely engaged, without arrogance. It is wonderful to talk to people and to be able to facilitate something ... it's a warm, fuzzy feeling. If you have made a lot of money you should give it away in your lifetime; it is the most enjoyable thing you can do, much better than buying a bigger yacht. The money goes such a long way. I can't imagine you could have so much fun ... I have had so much fun with all the organisations that we have funded, and learned such a lot from them.'

And he finally runs out of steam ...

Would that more people were like him.

→ www.aglimmerofhope.org

MICHAEL NORTON

I am in Pizza Express in Baker Street with Michael Norton. As I study the menu he is telling me how he has just come from the London Business School where a team of managers are developing one of his ideas – 'Say Neau to Bottled Water' (if you don't get it, say it!) – and how, if the campaign takes off, he hopes the profits will go to charity and how ridiculous it is that everyone drinks bottled water rather than good old tap water . . .

And we are off into two hours of ideas. For instance:

- All rich countries should adopt a poor country, similar to an enterprise zone. So Britain might, for example, get Kenya. All our companies would know about it and build their businesses and call centres there.
- There should be a 'Gift Aid laundering scheme' whereby you would register as a Gift Aid client at your bank and they would claim the Gift Aid for you and automatically pass it on to your chosen charity.
- Venture philanthropy is Good, as it allows people to give in a creative, longer term way. Large voluntary organisations are mostly Bad; half the money goes missing in one way or another.
- People have a great desire to help other people, but they don't know what to do and prefer small things where they can make a difference.
- There should be a Dragon's Den programme for charities.

And so on . . .

Michael Norton is intelligent, eccentric and very good fun. And he gets things done.

He founded the Directory of Social Change (www.dsc.org.uk), the Centre for Innovation in Voluntary Action (CIVA, www.civa.org.uk), Changemakers and YouthBank UK, and more recently was one of the founders of unLTD, the Foundation for Social Entrepreneurs, which received an endowment of £100 million from the Millennium Commission, and makes awards to over 1,000 individuals in the UK every year who wish to create change in their communities.

And he has written numerous books – the most interesting and entertaining of which is *365 Ways to Change the World* – how to make a better, fairer, freer, greener world every day. For 365 ideas buy the book or visit www.365ACT.com.

How to be a Philanthropist

Theresa Lloyd's book *Why Rich People Give* was the first UK research report into the attitudes towards philanthropy of wealthy people in the UK. The research identified five key motivators for giving:

1. Belief in the cause.
2. Being a catalyst for change.
3. The satisfaction of personal development and defining a place in history.
4. Duty and responsibility to those less fortunate.
5. The fun of being involved with a new range of people.

Which of these strikes a note with you? During my research for this book I discovered one more surprising motivation for philanthropy: anger. Many times I talked to people who have come across some injustice and become angry enough to take action. With others it is what the French call *'noblesse oblige'* – an underlying belief that wealth, power and prestige came with responsibilities. It is a moral obligation of those of high birth and in powerful social positions to act with kindness and generosity to the poorer sections of society.

Whatever the reasons, to begin developing your own philanthropy programme, start by having a look through the plan outlined in Chapter 3: How to Give to Charity (page 68), it sets out the necessary guidelines step by step. But there are several other things you should bear in mind if you are to take your giving to another perhaps more strategic level.

Impact

Many major givers now plan their giving in an increasingly effective manner. They are no longer happy just to write out a cheque to a charity, they want their donation to make a real impact on a particular problem, or cause, and in a charity's ability to improve and increase its effectiveness. Some focus on giving money to charities entering a critical stage of change in their development, one that will enable them to do even more work for their chosen client base. And it is exciting to be able to help 'enable' such growth.

Using the analytical skills normally used in finance and business, they try to understand how charities work and monitor the impact of their donation. They want to find exciting and worthwhile opportunities to give, in a variety of different areas, and give to the best organisations in that area. By committing to long-term funding of a cause, more along the lines of a partnership, it enables a charity to make a step change in its performance.

Interestingly new philanthropists do not often belong to

the 'I want every £1 that I give to charity to go to the cause' crowd. They are intelligent and thoughtful people who understand the difference that their gift could make and know that it costs money, time and good management to deliver the best possible benefit. They set aside a portion of their donation to ensure that this happens. They are happy to fund a new area of work that perhaps the charity couldn't risk setting aside funds to start. Or invest in improving the management or governance.

These new philanthropists, and the people who advise them should be encouraged, because they have decided to turn their brainpower, and not inconsiderable financial firepower, towards helping people less fortunate. Most major donors though have no idea how to find good destinations for their money, and many seek out experienced people with knowledge in different areas who know how to give money away effectively to causes that need it badly and will use it well. Useful partnerships can then be formed.

Every individual has different thoughts and views about what they want to do, how much money they are prepared to give, how much time they can spare and how involved they want to be. Giving your money to a cause and taking an interest in that cause is a very personal decision which touches your life values. Which is perhaps why you don't generally hear people talking about their charitable involvement, or how much they give, in public or amongst their friends.

When I am discussing giving with such donors I use different models each suited to the particular needs of the individual. I meet each person and discuss their current and recent giving, their interests and how much money they are prepared to give. I explain the tax benefits and discover how much time and involvement each person wants to put aside. It's called the 'audit' phase.

We then research a number of possible charities and projects, and present a shortlist of exciting, worthwhile and often innovative opportunities, which have been checked out by the most knowledgeable people working in the relevant area. The next step is to introduce the giver to the projects that they are interested in funding, 'light the touch paper and retire'. On a more serious note, this is an enormously exciting time, and the moment when great things are possible. Usually this is when the potential donors become both moved and enthused. Possibly the most interesting part of this whole process is finding lesser known smaller charities, all doing great work.

Use Your Head and Your Heart

Contrary to what you might have heard, people are not motivated to give because they see a piece of outstanding financial analysis. They give because something touches them personally, inspires them or makes them very angry. They give to causes they feel passionate about and to outstanding, inspirational people who lead various charities and have the ability to deliver progress and change – not just visualise it. It is simply life enhancing to be part of an organisation that is engaged in helping others.

To be a successful philanthropist, you have to engage your heart as well as your head. Effective philanthropy is about using your brain – and your human qualities, in reverse order. It is not all about leverage and outcomes. There is only a certain amount that financial analysis can tell you about the treatment of a heroin addict, the improvement in self-esteem of a young person, or the problems faced by a battered woman. It's often the unexpected results that make the difference – the ones you never thought of analysing in the first place. Profit is comparatively easy to measure but it is much harder to measure the 'outcomes' when running a hospice caring for the terminally ill. Without your heart engaged, you are going to crash hard when you meet people who are mentally ill, severely disabled, have been battered and beaten up, smell strongly because they are homeless, are depressed and lifeless after years on heroin.

The type A mentality, the results-driven mind that has made you a great success, is one thing but you need more. Someone once said that compassion is the opposite of competitiveness.

Much more to the point, those who care for people like this are of a completely different mindset to you. They are usually gentle, caring, dedicated, stressed, overworked and often poorly paid. Many of them are saints. During my period at Whizz-Kidz, I visited special needs schools, where severely disabled children with very impaired movement and speech, were looked after with enormous love and care. All day, every day, year in year out, by men and women who frankly must have been made on another planet. And it is the same in any world where real love, commitment and care is needed – a hospice, an old people's home, a cancer ward and so on.

These people march to a different drum. The fact that they don't understand cash flows, how to write three-year business plans, can't see the marketing opportunities available if they had more money does not, repeat not, make them incompetent. You wouldn't know how to give palliative care to a young woman dying of cancer. And they wouldn't dream of telling you how to run your office.

You need to be quiet, supportive, humble and gentle. Human.

Cash Rich and Time Poor

Many major donors are cash rich and time poor. They can give significant sums quickly and they understand the impact it will make. But they don't have time for meetings, waffle and philosophical discussion. That said, however busy we are, we can always make the time available for the things we want to do, to see the people we want to meet. And an hour or so out during the week to visit a charity or good cause can provide a very welcome break from the grief and pressure of the day job.

You may be too busy to help as much as you would like now, and not have time for involvement. On the other hand increasingly people who are able to make large donations to charities do want to become involved in the progress and work of the organisation they are supporting.

Would you like to attend the charity's events? Or even put on one for them? Would you like to see first hand the work they do? (Most charities will happily show you round their offices and the projects they run; this is by far the best bit!) Are you able to lend support in kind, for example by seconding someone in your company (with their agreement!) to help the organisation's management? (Whizz-Kidz had many offers of support like this, including a review of our risk management by Marsh, and the redesign of our website by a great group from Reed Elsevier PLC.)

Are you the mentoring type? Mentoring the CEO of a

charity or the headmaster or headmistress of a school could be invaluable to them. Leadership is a very lonely business and an outside voice can bring calm and practical help. Do you want to go on the charity's Board of Trustees and take an active part in the governance of the organisation? (As you might do if you were a major investor in a private company.)

What Sort of Feedback Do You Expect?

You have discovered a fabulous cause, run by people you trust and who inspire you, and given them some significant funding to help their work, or to start a risky new initiative. The results have real impact on people's lives. Now what? Leaving aside the obvious fact that they *should* thank you, treat you as an adult and with real reverence, how much do you care about how the money is used? How often do you want to be updated?

In my experience, some charities are hugely inept at thanking donors, and even worse at keeping them in the loop. The way forward is to start as you mean to go on. If you are in constant contact with a charity and involved in some areas of their work, you will probably know what is going on. At the very least it is not a bad policy to ask the CEO or a director to come and see you once a year for forty-five minutes and give you an update on the progress of the project. No one has really got time for endless reports these days!

I particularly like the approach of a major foundation, which asks people who want a grant or donation for a particular project to put it down on paper. They must include how much they want, why they need that amount, how long their project is going to take to implement, who is going to manage it and how, what the results will be and who will benefit. They then have to come and meet the manager and trustees of the foundation in person and explain their case. I like this approach because passion usually shines through. If they receive a grant they have to return within a year for forty-five minutes and report on their progress.

On the other hand a very wise friend suggested that once you have found the cause you wish to help, you should visit them, give them the cheque and leave them in peace. His argument is that your money is very unlikely to be wasted by passionate people.

The Family

Do you wish to involve members of your family in philanthropy? Depending on the family, it can be a very positive endeavour. It brings people together, gives them a joint interest to be debated and decided, and perhaps most powerfully introduces children to the whole issue of 'giving something back'. In America, families often put their children on the boards of the family charitable foundation, making them responsible for helping to give away their family's wealth.

The importance of families in philanthropy, and women in particular, is not to be underestimated. Yes, some wealthy wives do spend a very large part of their lives shopping and eating things surrounded by rocket, and doing a little light charity ball work, semi-oblivious to the surrounding world. But most are much, much wiser. Not only do they often have the time to research causes but they are often much more intelligent and intuitive about key social problems. And many of them are formidable fundraisers. They are also increasingly concerned about the upbringing of their children in a privileged world. Women and families I have met to discuss charity/philanthropy matters have concerns for their children that roughly fall into two camps.

There are more young, rich teenage children than you would believe who can only be described as dysfunctional. Caught up between being a member of a hugely wealthy family with the highest aspirations for their offspring, and a sometimes almost wilful lack of love and attention from their 'frantically busy' parents – they get truly bolshy, taking normal teenage rebellion to a completely new level. There is strangely almost surreal common ground between these young people and young people from the poorest housing estates.

But then there are the wiser parents who know full well that life in a Lear Jet is no foundation for a sensible life – and who genuinely want their young to grow up with a sense of values.

These two groups of young people are fascinating and full of potential. I have never met a young person from a privileged background who isn't fundamentally moved when taken aside quietly and introduced to the work of a charity. Whether it is helping the homeless, visiting an addiction centre, meeting disadvantaged young people – they log on quickly and get involved. It doesn't change their lives or often their behaviour overnight – but it does introduce them to the idea of travelling through life with the knowledge than many others are less fortunate than themselves. And for the ones who one day will inherit significant money rather than earning it, this has got to be positive.

Setting Up a Charitable Trust

Setting up your own charitable trust or foundation – it's the same thing – allows you to plan your charitable giving in a more methodical manner. Creating a foundation allows you to create an enduring fund, which could last beyond your lifetime. The trust would allow you to decide how you want to use some of your own taxes, and the destination of your money, rather than allow the government to do it.

You can choose the aims of the charity, whether it is to help organisations or individuals, or operate in other areas of the world. You can choose its name and trustees, and also take advantage of the many different tax benefits. For example, a charitable trust receives the normal tax relief benefits, but also doesn't pay corporation or inheritance tax, or tax on any investment income. It is your bat and ball and game, and, managed properly, could make a significant impact on a corner of the world and live on after you.

Many people involve their families in the whole process. You can make your children trustees if they are over eighteen, which is an excellent and increasingly popular way of introducing them to the world of effective philanthropy, to say nothing of encouraging their involvement in helping others and in the decision-making processes. The only real disadvantage is that a trust is required to produce a formal report and accounts each year, and send the Charity Commission an annual return.

Your accountant or solicitor will help you draw up the

necessary paperwork, and register with the Charity Commission. Charities Aid Foundation (CAF) operates a simple, effective scheme for creating your own trust account, which they then help administer and can be managed anonymously, i.e. you will not get direct applications. The only disadvantage is that whilst you would be involved in the decision-making and control the charitable giving, the trustees are the CAF trustees. The CAF scheme gives you the opportunity to concentrate on your charitable giving - the result is that you have the facilities normally associated with a private charitable trust but without the responsibility for the usual accounting and administrative burdens.

If you want to focus your giving in a specific community or area, you can operate in partnership with a local Community Foundation Network, which knows the local needs well. Useful websites: www.cafonline.org; www.communityfoundations.org.uk.

Many foundations are started by wealthy and intelligent people who, rather than just lob in a donation to one cause or another, have taken the matter into their own hands, and set out to look for 'partners' doing great work, which they then support and encourage to make a real difference. These new foundations want to 'add value', are very focused and are to be encouraged.

ARK

ARK (Absolute Return for Kids) was started in 2002 by some well-known names in the hedge fund industry 'to transform the lives of children who are victims of abuse, disability, illness and poverty'. Crucially ARK doesn't 'donate' or 'give the money away'. They 'invest' it themselves in causes which they have thoroughly researched and where they feel that their donation and involvement will make a real impact, importantly 'measuring the outcome' of their work.

And they have money. This is 'hedge fund land' where the sums earned by successful managers enter stratospheric realms. ARK is most well known in charity and media circles for hosting an annual ball that regularly raises astonishing sums of money in one evening. Their last annual dinner in May 2007 raised £26.6 million. No, you weren't misreading it, over £26 million in one evening. Behind the glamour and the glittering auction prizes, the real heroes of the evening are the original founders, patrons and commercial sponsors who actually donate most of the money. They also cover all the central administration costs of the charity so that 100 per cent of the money raised goes to the people who need help. It is a sobering fact that the 1000 guests, who include some hugely wealthy people many of whom could write out cheques for substantial sums themselves, contribute considerably less than the founders and sponsors.

ARK focus on three core themes: combating HIV/AIDS; the delivery of quality education; and implementing deinstitutionalisation by closing orphanages.

The HIV/AIDS programme in South Africa has prevented just under 30,000 children from becoming orphans and provides retroviral drugs to 14,000 mothers and carers. Retovirals can turn HIV into a chronic rather than an acute illness and reduce the transmission rate dramatically.

Working with another charity, Hope and Homes for

Children, ARK has successfully closed seven orphanages in Romania transforming the lives of 1,650 children. (The conditions in which these children lived were truly appalling.) They are now embarking on a programme to close orphanages in Bulgaria, three institutions in the next three years.

In September 2006 they opened the first of at least twelve planned Academy schools. Academies 'are partnerships between the Department for Education and Skills, the local authority and a sponsor'. Publicly funded for the most part but independently governed. The issue of Academies is still controversial. The Government has identified 200 of the worst performing schools in the UK, where 30 per cent or less of the pupils achieve 5 GCSE passes at A–C level. Even in 2007 many children leave school without basic numeracy and literacy skills, and in many schools there is a correlation between the proportion of children who get free meals (the poorer children) and lower GCSE attainment. The Government is committed to turning these schools into academies, run and partially financed by 'the private' sector.

Burlington Danes is one such Academy. A 'faith school' in White City, West London, it has an open admissions policy and 850 pupils. ARK took over the school in September 2006 when it had just come out of 'special measures', Government 'speak' for under-performing schools with serious problems.

Stanley Fink, one of ARK's founders and trustees, gave ARK £500,000 to support its general education programme and £1.5 million to Burlington Danes specifically. The Government contributed £15 million. The total of £16.5m is all being spent on new buildings/refurbishment of the existing buildings – a basic premise of the Academy programme is that academies should operate with exactly the same funding as any other maintained school.

ARK's approach to its Academy programme is enlightened: they want to lift the aspirations and choices of all the children and young people, not just to focus on just the brightest and the best pupils, So that every child can leave school at the age of sixteen, or preferably eighteen, with higher personal aspirations and real choices in terms of qualifications, that would enable them to go on to higher education or a better job.

→ www.arkonline.org

Impetus Trust – Venture Philanthropy

I was rather sceptical about venture philanthropy. Not least because of the comparatively small amount of money coming into charities via this route.

But in the course of researching this book I spent some time talking with Nat Sloane, one of the founders of Impetus Trust, and also looked at some of the interesting charities in which they have 'invested'. I now think that venture philanthropy could prove to be a good model for serious donors to use in their own charitable giving.

Stephen Dawson was one of the first venture equity investors in the UK and Nat Sloane was a successful entrepreneur, venture capitalist and management consultant. They were both regular donors to charities, but had no real sense of where their money was actually going, or what it was being used for. With their venture capital background, they wanted to know that giving their time or money would make a difference and enable a charity to make a step change in its performance.

At issue was the way that charities and funders worked together or, rather, often didn't. Stephen, Nat and their colleagues felt that there was an opportunity to provide longer term, strategic and more engaged funding. Their involvement would include financing a charity's infrastructure, hands-on management support and capacity building delivered through projects run by volunteer associates.

People in the corporate sector would be encouraged to take a role, not only working with the charity but supporting its management. New donors and others joining the sector from the business world would also be able to provide 'impetus' and a fresh look at a charity's operation.

They were prepared to commit sensible sums of money – between £250,000 and £500,000 – to their chosen charities during the term of the partnership.

They began to look for interesting charities which were at a critical point of change in their growth, led by great CEOs who had the vision, energy and enterprise and, importantly, the ability to deliver the organisation's plans.

The founders and a small group of wealthy donors contributed an initial fund of £3 million. Impetus has now raised £8 million and invested in nine 'interesting and different' charities. They are currently raising another fund of £30 million.

In the world of charitable giving this is small beer, but to a medium-size charity it is a lot of money, and, critically, provides stable funding and involvement and support. It is also a relief to find a group of sensible people who want to give and are prepared to roll up their sleeves to help rather than just 'donate'.

→ www.impetustrust.org

When St Giles approached Impetus for investment, it was primarily a day centre working with homeless people. It was also experimenting with a range of services including one involved in training prisoners to provide housing advice to the wider population at Wandsworth prison. St Giles understood the reality that one-third of the 120,000 entering prison and two-thirds leaving prison had housing issues and that stable housing was integral to reducing re-offending. St Giles had developed a 'peer advisory' model that was distinctive and cost-effective. It also looked like a model that could be expanded into other prisons and form the basis for services within and beyond prison.

The key point on which St Giles differed from other charities was its direct work with prisoners and ex-offenders, and this has been the focus of its step change since it formed a three-year partnership with Impetus in November 2004.

St Giles is now able to deliver a range of services which engage with offenders as early as possible, and which enables them to access housing, support services, and training/employment, in order to avoid re-offending. Prisoners are now able to study for an NVQ Level 3 in Advice and Guidance (equivalent to two A-levels) and advise their peers on things many people take for granted, such as how to fill in job applications and plan for an interview, as well as preparing for any prejudices they may face on leaving prison.

St Giles has also significantly broadened its reach.

From working in just two prisons they are now linked to almost two dozen, as well as beginning work in young offenders' institutions. Since the partnership began, St Giles has tripled its income, increased the peer advisers fivefold – and the number of ex-offenders placed in employment tenfold – and found accommodation for nine times as many people as before. Starting from a base in South East London, St Giles is now a major player in prisoner and ex-offender services across London and the south-east of England.

Impetus worked with St Giles on business planning, performance management, management development and market positioning, then on strengthening the management and governance for a rapidly growing organisation.

New Philanthropy Capital – The Researchers

New Philanthropy Capital was started by a team of four City financiers who wanted to encourage philanthropy from wealthy donors, and to act as a bridge to charities by using the analytical skills that they applied in the financial and business world to research a charity's effectiveness. Their starting point was spot on. Numerous if not all charities are searching for new donors, and generally potential donors only know about the larger or better known ones. They lack any real knowledge of the great variety of interesting smaller charities needing support, where their money could make a much bigger impact.

In 2006 NPC actively advised on grants to the tune of £10 million and their aim for 2007 is £15 million, which doesn't include its consultancy work. Its research has produced several very good reports on areas as diverse as domestic violence, cancer in the UK, and disabled children and their families.

It also publishes a list of fact sheets on individual charities, which have all been visited and thoroughly researched. These reports are an excellent starting point if you are looking to donate sensibly, and are available free online when you register on the website.

NPC has grown and improved over the past couple of years. It is, in my view, still too focused on 'return on investment' rather than 'generosity of spirit', and some argue that investing in 'well-run charities' is hardly rocket science, and that you could lead donors to help charities that are doing great work but are not as 'effective' as they could or should be. But NPC is an intelligent organisation and doing a very good job.

→ www.philanthropycapital.org

And Finally ...

Now you are engaged, hopefully mentally and emotionally. You are in a position to learn, contribute and make a difference, to understand a charity's finances, share its triumphs and successes, and empathise with its problems and challenges.

Becoming actively involved in a cause will enrich your life in many ways. You will make new friends. You will moan less about your lot in life. You will feel useful. You will learn more and more about the cause or causes you've joined.

PHILANTHROPY

You can politely refuse requests to support all other charities with a clear conscience. You have made your decisions and are excited and enthused by your chosen causes. In future you can simply respond to all incoming requests that you have carefully thought through your charitable giving and work, you have decided to contribute to X, Y and Z and you try to do as much as you can to help them. You know that the request comes from an excellent and worthwhile cause and you wish them success, but a man/woman can only do so much. You are free!

Chapter 6

CORPORATE GIVING

'I always say that there are three types of people in life – those who do nothing, those who talk about it, and those who get on and do it. At M&S we are doers. We can't promise that we will always get it right – we are not perfect – but we are sincere in our intentions and determined to do our bit to help make a difference.'
Stuart Rose, CEO Marks & Spencer PLC

What are we to make of the very low levels of corporate giving in the UK? How much companies and businesses actually GIVE to charities and their communities?

According to Charities Aid Foundation, the top 500 companies in Britain in 2006–7 made pre-tax profits of £169 billion, and gave away on average 0.2 per cent, around £1.1 billion. Of this £400 million is actual cash, the rest is gifts in kind and volunteering hours. A few enlightened companies give 1 per cent of their annual profits. A few heroes such as Sainsbury (7.2 per cent), ITV (6.2 per cent) and Northern Rock (5 per cent) give more. The majority of donations came from the FTSE 100 companies who gave £986 million or 90 per cent of the total. This is still only 0.8 per cent of their combined pre-tax profits. And the lion's share of the total giving – 27 per cent – came from GlaxoSmithKline.

CORPORATE GIVING

All in all, company donations account for only 4.3 per cent of the total income received by charities in 2006-7. (The contrast with corporate giving in America is stark. In the USA recent figures show donations by companies at $12.7 billion, nearly FIVE times the levels in the UK.)

Translated into hard cash this means that a company making £1 million pre-tax profit a year gives £2,000 to charity. From their *profits*. Which leaves precisely £998,000 left to reinvest or pay to their shareholders or in bonuses. One per cent would be – put your hand up if I am going too quickly – £10,000, leaving only £990,000.

And it gets better, or worse, depending on how you are feeling at the moment! A donation to charity is classed as a business expense, so Corporation tax can be saved. Currently this is 30 per cent. So if a company gives £2,000 it will only actually cost it £1,400. If it gives £10,000 it will only cost £7,000. From a million.

Given this, you might, as an ordinary person, imagine that persuading companies to give even 1 per cent of the profits to charities would be a cakewalk, but you would be horribly wrong. After nearly twenty years of trying to persuade companies to donate 1 per cent of their pre-tax profits into their community in the form of cash donations, employee time and community programme management costs, even Business in the Community (www.bitc.org.uk) has finally flung in the towel. It has 'repositioned' its Percent Club, and folded it into a new programme called the 'Community Mark', an award scheme 'to identify companies that are good investors in the community'. This, with the blessing of the Prince of Wales and Gordon Brown, and a reasonably good list of the great and the good in British business lined up in support.

It is enough to make you weep, especially given the desperate need charities have for new income and the enormous increase in the value of companies and in corporate wealth over the corresponding period. Support from corporates is highly prized – it usually arrives more easily, quickly and with less strings attached than government funding. The role of the 'third sector' in combating disadvantage and building a more cohesive society has never been more important. Yet its ability to play this vital role is undermined by financial fragility: 'It is fragmented, undercapitalised and, in aggregate, unable to invest in sustainable growth and development.' (Social Investment Bank report, March 2007)

TOP 10 COMPANIES IN TERMS OF DONATIONS

GlaxoSmithKline PLC
BP PLC
Royal Bank of Scotland Group (The) PLC
Rio Tinto PLC
Barclays PLC
HSBC Holdings PLC
BHP Billiton PLC
Vodafone Group PLC
Lloyds TSB Group PLC
Northern Rock PLC

Source: Charities Aid Foundation: Charity Trends, 2007

But this is not just about 'big business'. There are an estimated 4.4 million businesses in the UK, 99 per cent small, with fewer than fifty employees. Imagine what would happen if every business in the country was asked, encouraged or just cajoled into giving away 1 per cent of their pre-tax profits – read disposable income – and investing it in their communities or giving it to charities. Never mind the serious tax break – although the Government could help here by giving companies more tax incentives.

The total amount that could be raised would amount to billions of additional income to charities each year and the impact on society would be simply colossal. And imagine the positive social impact of this active engagement by companies and their employees on the fabric of this country.

In the next five years I believe every company in the country should have a sensible charity programme as part of their business plan. One that engages its employees and helps the community in which it lives and works. Employees want it, customers expect it and shareholders are catching up.

In my opinion, an enlightened approach to the community in which you work makes financial sense for companies. It is of benefit to the company, its employees, its shareholders and the members of its community.

Anita Roddick, founder of Body Shop, who gave £1 million to Amnesty to help fund their new Human Rights Centre in East London, wrote an article for the *Financial Times* in which she urged businesses to plough back some their wealth into the community. She described Body Shop as 'a great business experiment' which is still proving a point: that you can run an entrepreneurial business and provide a return to shareholders while campaigning on ethical issues and placing a high value on human capital.

In December 2005 she announced that she would give away her fortune, worth some £51 million.

> *If you think you are too small to have an impact, try going to bed with a mosquito.*
> This quotation, by American writer Philip Elmer-DeWitt, is displayed on the side of the Body Shop trucks in England and was one of Anita Roddick's favourites. People often say that one person cannot make a difference: Roddick did.

People who don't get this, the 'I work to maximise the returns to my shareholders' brigade, are in for a horrible shock as their competitors actively engage with charities and gain real management and marketing advantage.

Let's deal with the question of why companies and businesses in Britain don't give first, before explaining how a more enlightened approach could help them run a more intelligent business, improve profitability, and at the same time radically transform the income of charities in Britain, thus helping the weaker members of society.

We'd Like To But . . .

Many senior executives would genuinely like their company to give to good causes, and would be thrilled and excited to be able to make a 'social' difference. But they don't really understand that pro-active support for good causes and the development of a serious charity programme will help them manage their business more effectively and enhance shareholder value.

Many completely misunderstand the phrase 'corporate

giving'. The very words set them on edge, because they think that they are being asked to give away part of their company's annual profit to a good cause, which they don't honestly feel that they should or can do. The shareholders would complain.

In reality, their contribution should be to lead by example, giving to create an enthusiasm for giving throughout their company, which will enable their business to make a real and valuable contribution to the community in which it operates, and potentially raise huge sums for charity. Their task is to encourage their staff to raise money for a chosen charity and either match the staff's financial contributions – or donate a significant sum towards priming the charity programme (for example, ensuring that all the money the staff raise goes directly to the cause). This financial contribution must also implicitly recognise the enormous business benefits of running a powerful and effective partnership with their chosen charity.

There are real and tangible advantages to this approach. And if you are in a management position in a company I hope you will find the case history and business profiles interesting. These are all companies where the adoption of a charity programme has <u>definitely</u> improved their business, and they have remained extremely profitable!

Our Shareholders

One of the most often repeated arguments given by CEOs and directors of publicly owned companies against giving money to good causes is as follows: 'If you work in a privately owned business, and your directors or partners decide to give money away, it is their business. They can do anything they like with their own money, from buying a private plane to making large donations to charity. If you run a public company, however, you are not paid to give shareholders' money away. The shareholders and institutions are the investors who own the business, and you are paid to manage the business as well as possible and maximise the return in the form of a dividend. It is up to the shareholders to choose how they wish to distribute their own earnings.'

Put another way, if you accept that in a privately owned business, the managers should not give money away without asking the owners, then in a public company you shouldn't give money away without asking the shareholders. It is their money.

There are shades of 'we are only following orders' about this argument, as though the directors of such companies consider charitable giving to be off limits. Some of my best business friends believe it to be a) true and b) unarguable. I have discussed with them the fact that the business must have a wider *raison d'être* in the twenty-first century, and I am happy report that some have begun to see that there might be a case for a more enlightened approach. The arguments for using engaged charity programmes to improve staff morale and internal communication proved particularly persuasive. (How many of your employees know who the company chairman is, never mind more than a dozen colleagues?)

Which is exciting. Most consumers and staff would say that a business has a social responsibility to behave well and take an active interest in their world, and would love the businesses they work for, and buy from, to give generously to charities. But lots of business leaders of public

CORPORATE GIVING

companies are not yet there. Of course the shareholders in a business are very important, because they provide the capital and investment for the company to grow. But all stakeholders – staff, suppliers, customers and often government – are now increasingly recognised as equally important.

Perhaps both groups, shareholders and stakeholders, should actually be asking the companies what they are doing to be useful. How much *are* they giving? To whom? Why?

Morally: 'We expect you to be an active, open and generous contributor to your community and we insist that you set aside a percentage of the profits to invest in the communities in which most of your employees work.' This is a world where an extra £1 million spent wisely would make a major impact on a community or a cause, and hardly register on the shareholders' dividend payment.

And managerially: 'Are you doing anything in any area of our business that could put the business at a competitive risk and undermine its future?' This is the world of risk management and it is now as much about how a company behaves – financially, ethically, socially and about its relationship with the environment.

If some of the major pension funds were to put their foot down, and use their enormous influence to ensure that the companies in which they invest look after the communities in which they work, enormous social gain would be made throughout the country.

The remarkable thing is that there is a sensible and compelling case for linking up with a charity or a cause and giving it money and other forms of support.

What Do Charities Really Want?

OK. Let's try to keep this simple. What do you think charities need most?

That's right, money! And best of all, unrestricted money – to fund their overheads, fund a new post, a new project and the less 'popular' bits of their work.

A company can provide this much-needed money by adopting a charity and encouraging its employees to create a fundraising programme and matching their efforts. (It might even save the company real money from paying out for unsolicited donations.)

Employee volunteering schemes offering groups of staff to a charity to paint the walls of a youth centre are good, but not the main meal.

While I was writing the book one savvy charity CEO remarked that the East End of London was overrun with investment bankers, lawyers, accountants and insurance folk doing 'good work', and while it is hard to be hard on them for doing it, it's impossible to feel that they couldn't find better ways to use their talents to help a project – such as organising a fundraising event for it.

Some volunteer schemes do deliver enormous good. Others are simply part of a firewall. If a company can say that it has a charity committee, with a volunteering scheme focused on education, or a nearby deprived area, then requests for donations from charities can be deflected from the directors. Teams of employee volunteers take time off to mentor children, paint the walls of community centres and much more. All this does have a value and shows that the company cares. But the subject of money is often mysteriously left out of the process.

One businessman I know told me that he would rather pay £500 *not* to paint walls in an East End school, and instead focused his time on reading and improving the business plans of young people on the Prince's Trust business start-up scheme. He feels it is a much more relevant use of his skills. Another successful investment banker came from modest background and returned to his old secondary school to help out financially, and to act as a mentor to the current headmaster.

What Can Companies Do for Charities?

After giving money, intelligent companies offer to invest in building the capacity of a charity to enhance or grow its work, to make a bigger impact.

They can fund a new position that will strengthen the charity's work. A brand new service – something the charity would love to do but can't – because it would be to risky. A new database. Help with IT. Help with HR. A marketing programme or a new brand. Redesigning the charity's website. A secondment of a member of staff. Provide premises or grounds for an event.

A company has its own centre of influence. It can enlist the help of its staff, its suppliers and of course its customers to help its chosen cause. The key issue is to enable the charity to do great work. In itself, this is hugely motivational, inspiring and worthwhile.

The Business Case for Giving

It is not good enough to wail on about this. We need to put forward a good business case for giving more. Maybe if the staff and the customers of a company ask it to be more generous towards charities, while competitors and peers start giving more, then things would change.

Giving brings many benefits to *your* business. But before you start reading this, just pause for a moment and imagine what would happen if your company were to *give* money, and inspire your company's employees to fundraise for, and use their talents to help a charity. Imagine how much more enjoyable and satisfying their jobs would be, and the sort of things the whole group of intelligent, motivated people could do to help the poor, the disadvantaged, the elderly, the sick, the planet ...

The Case for Corporate Generosity

A good charity programme will bring the following benefits to a company:

1. *Unites different businesses within a group*
A sensible charitable giving programme establishes a set of core values and a consistent business philosophy across a company with which people can identify and take pride in. It brings people working in different 'silos' together and unites national offices throughout the country, and the world, to work round a common non-business theme. (See Reed Elsevier page 231.)

2. *Encourages better communication between employees*
It improves internal communications between all employees and directors of a company. Working together on community, charity and fundraising activities breaks down barriers, helps teambuilding, is positive and motivating. It

links employees and clients around a common and non-commercially competitive theme, and provides great opportunities for social involvement and interaction. People who play together stay together.

3. Inspires employees
People want to work for a company that has a value system, especially graduates. They don't come to work just for the money. A well-developed and effective giving programme is proactive, positive, inspiring and rewarding for everyone in the company. It helps to build a positive working environment and pride in the company: 'We are doing our job *and* doing something useful to help "our" community, using the assets of "our" company.' (See Innocent Drinks page 223.)

4. Improves job satisfaction
Supporting a charity or cause through volunteering adds variety to an employee's job, teaches them new skills not normally learned or even necessary in their job, and improves job satisfaction enormously. This may appear a 'softer' reward but it is actually one of the key benefits. Rather then just battling through the day job, people also have an opportunity to make a difference.

It allows a company's employees to use their talent, time and skills to help those less fortunate than themselves, in a manner that can produce real impact. Practically, you can encourage your employees to be useful by giving them time off to help out in a local project, mentor a young person in a school or paint a community centre. Managerially you can help by lending your brainpower, or the talent within your business to help a cause. Lawyers can give pro bono advice; advertising and PR firms can lend their creative talents and buying power; the IT people can help design a website; the HR people can help with training and best employment practices.

Having this genuine extra dimension in your business helps to attract and retain the best people in a competitive recruiting environment. (See Richer Sounds page 226.)

5. *Generates goodwill in the community where you have a presence*
Ensuring local customer loyalty and easier recruitment of staff.

6. *More customers!*
Happy, committed and valued employees make happy, committed and valuable customers.

Everyone involved in customer service knows that effective customer service has to begin with your own staff. They must know what they are doing, and they must also feel fairly treated, remunerated, involved and as positive as they can be about life given that they have to work rather than travel the world. First class customer service leads directly to better sales.

Unless the workplace is a good place, any serious attempts to make the world a better place won't work well, or as well as they could. In my softer moments at Whizz-Kidz I used to quietly encourage everyone to care for each other, since their job ultimately involved caring for disabled children. Walk the talk. (See M&S page 229.)

7. *Reputation*
What price reputation? One CEO of a public company I spoke to felt that a good reputation accounted for a small

but significant part of his company's share price. A great deal of money, and much more than the cost of an excellent charity programme.

8. Good investment
An enlightened charity programme is a very good investment. A proactive approach is completely consistent with enhancing shareholder value. In fact, not doing it properly puts your company a) at risk on several fronts, b) at a serious competitive disadvantage. And your shareholders will not be at all pleased.

9. A more intelligent business
If a charity programme is closely related to what a company really understands it can inform and educate the company. One of the best known examples of this process is from B&Q. An enquiry from a *Sunday Times* journalist in the early 1990s about the sources of timber used by the company prompted it to undertake research into their purchasing systems and supply chain. Given the remarkable range of wood products sold by the company – from brooms to garden sheds – this proved a major exercise and took time. It led however to the formation of the Forest Stewardship Council and the eventual sourcing of all B&Q's wood and paper products from either well-managed forests or recycled material. Buyers were 'sold' the policy and customers gained confidence in the company. Similar commitments to reducing the amount of packaging on their products, monitoring and labelling the level of chemicals in items such as garden pesticides and paint, and actively reducing the impact of the business operation on climate change are now part of their social responsibility

programme (see www.diy.com/socialresponsibility).

10. Better customer relationships

Customers, consumers, or whatever you want to call us, are much smarter these days than we used to be. Our perception of value, quality and customer service is much higher than before, we are much more vociferous and we can smell deceit, spin and bullshit.

Given a choice we would rather purchase a product or a service from a company we admire, which treats us well, which we feel is well run and 'has a life' over and above making as much money as possible. A company that is behaving properly and contributing to its own community. In plain language, we will give it our money, rather than another business with a poor reputation that doesn't give a toss about the way it behaves. This means a real increase in income for those who care. Think Ben and Jerry's ice cream company, famously set up by two 'hippies' who took a $5 correspondence course in ice cream making, and ended up with a multi-million dollar business. On the way they established a foundation which gave 7.5 per cent of pre-tax profits to charity.

The fact that some businesses seem to thrive while behaving miserably misses the point. Which is that if they behaved in a grown-up, responsible manner they would benefit even more. Seven in ten British adults think industry and commerce do not pay enough attention to their social responsibilities. (Source: The Public's Views of Corporate Responsibility, Mori 2005)

11. Marketing and public relations

There are significant marketing and media opportunities

to be gained by aligning your company with a charity or cause. The local newspaper or radio station may be less than excited about your new product or business initiative but they will generally be much more supportive and publicise the good work being done by your company and its employees in the community, which is publicly enhancing the reputation of the company.

Whizz-Kidz has large files of positive PR stories involving most of its corporate clients, mostly along the lines of the company's staff doing something mildly heroic or daft to provide mobility equipment for a local disabled child. This sort of press coverage can be worth serious money, and would not be obtainable through the company's normal business activities.

Adopting the right charity can help to develop a particular image for a company – association with funding schools and education projects, sports activity, the elderly, a medical cause or arts organisations.

12. *Networking*

Non-commercial events and activities, arranged to support a cause or charity, provide excellent networking opportunities for company executives to meet socially with current and potential clients. This is subtler behaviour than corporate entertainment at high-profile sports events – you are going to end up paying for the fun but at least the money goes to a good cause. Even charity balls at their worst are making an effort to help their cause, in spite of the fact that most of them actually make little money.

13. *Pure Philanthropy!*

If you run a business that is profitable, why on earth

wouldn't you *want* to give a small percentage to charitable causes, to help people who are less well off? Even if it is only 1 per cent. How about 10 per cent?

How to Plan an Effective Giving Programme

Time and again, while researching this book, I came across exceptional people who wanted to encourage their peers and employees to give: Sir Crispin Davis's leadership in establishing real corporate responsibility at Reed Elsevier; Julian Richer's pathfinding entrepreneurial approach to helping charities at Richer Sounds; the passion of Richard Reed and his colleagues at Innocent Drinks; and many others.

All these people build thought for the world into their businesses and want to encourage their employees to give. Some, like Julian, have offered to talk to other businesses about their positive experiences. Others have asked me to talk to their colleagues and employees about the importance of giving, and advise them how to do so practically and effectively.

I have been personally involved over a number of years with successful charity programmes with companies such as HSBC, M&S, Argos, Woolworths, Lunn Poly, Marsh, easyJet, Bestinvest and many others. They work, exceedingly well. And are fun. And are fruitful beyond belief.

These, then, are the essential ingredients for a successful charity programme. But first you need a plan. Set realistic targets, but ones that you hope you will beat. Pay particular attention to involving everyone in the company, and launching the programme successfully. What you need to focus on is the impact that you can make on a charity's work.

1. *Leadership from the top*

Personal commitment from the top of the company is absolutely critical for the success of a charity programme. The CEO has to 'own' the process, otherwise any generous and well-meaning initiatives will die on the vine. It's an opportunity for real leadership, as employees always look to the boss of a company to see what he wants to happen.

You have to decide that you wish your company to give to charity and to be usefully involved in the community in which it lives and works. For the moment we are not going to include recycling your paper, treating your employees fairly, behaving in a civilised manner to your suppliers, anything to do with health and safety, equal opportunities and all similar activities. We are going to place all of this under the heading of good management.

What we are talking about is additional proactive involvement and funding of causes and activities that help make the world a better place for future generations. Setting aside a percentage of your annual pre-tax profits for good causes, and a commitment to encourage your employees to involve themselves in good works.

Over several years building up Whizz-Kidz, I was fortunate to work with many excellent companies and senior business people. I met some truly inspiring individuals working in these companies, all of whom went out of their way to help raise staggering sums of money to provide mobility for disabled children. The moments when these people met the children they were supporting are amongst my very best memories.

2. *Aligned to business goals*
The best charity partnerships succeed when the company's

business goals are aligned with the right charity. Corporate giving should be strategic. The challenge is to invest money and resources in work that will be useful and fruitful, and that will enhance the company's reputation amongst its various audiences. Reputation equals value equals income.

It is important to establish what the chief executive, other senior directors and even the chairman wish to gain from developing an effective giving programme, because unless the senior management is committed to corporate responsibility, it will remain a Cinderella activity and will not work.

The directors shouldn't choose the charity programmes that the company decides to support, but they should help to define the areas of interest.

Then, together with those involved in the company's charity programme and other employees, they should identify benefits desired for the company and establish a clear plan. A year later, have they done what they set out to do?

3. *Effectively managed*

Select a manager to drive the charity programme. The person chosen should be senior and have clout, not just enthusiastic, energetic, personable and efficient. A lot will depend on their ability to enthuse members of the staff to volunteer as members of the charity committee and to persuade the bosses that a new fundraising venture should be undertaken or special project supported. They should report to the CEO or a senior director so that everyone knows that the programme matters and the boss is watching. The first step is to create a charity committee or group of 'charity champions', people drawn from within the company and representing each office or area of business.

4. Communications

Devise an internal communication plan, to tell everyone what is going on and what the practical results of their efforts are. You should also brief the marketing and PR people to tell everyone from the media to your customers what you are up to, why and what they can do to help you. You would be surprised at how little attention is given to this aspect of giving. Some of the largest companies in Britain, who donate large sums of money and are hugely committed to community charity or cultural work are woeful at telling anyone about it. Their own staff don't know what the company is doing, their customers don't know, and neither do the general public. BT recently won the top award from Business in the Community: Responsible Company of the Year. Have you any idea what they do for charity, for the community or for society?

5. Carry out an audit

Carry out an audit of all current and recent charity activities and initiatives throughout the company, including, if appropriate, subsidiaries and all divisions. How much money has been raised and given away in total? How was it raised? Who was it given to? Was it given tax effectively? Did the charity thank the company or the individuals who contributed? What was the impact? Was it fun and enjoyable?

What is the current level of volunteering in the company? Is there a payroll-giving scheme in place for employees? Does the company operate a matched giving scheme? Does everyone (or anyone) understand the tax breaks?

Importantly, you need to find out what works, or has worked, and what does not. What benefit and recognition did the company get from its contribution and work? Is the programme inspiring? Does it motivate the employees or is everyone just going through the motions? Is charity support virtually non-existent or subject to the whims of a senior few within the organisation? Or a relatively junior CSR post who has no real power to change the status quo?

Once the audit is complete you can start to develop a more reasoned approach. In some cases it is possible to create a few simple improvements that will have a significant impact. And an added benefit is that you can now politely refuse the majority of requests for donations, arguing that you now have a well thought-out charity programme that has the support of your directors and staff.

6. *Research and shortlist causes*

Giving money away effectively is very often more difficult than raising it in the first place. Having decided the area in which the company would like to give its support, the next task is to research and shortlist a number of possible charities, and ask them to present to the charity committee.

There are rules for this sort of process.

The potential charities or causes should be able to say why they need the company's support, what impact this support will make and what benefit the company will get from their involvement in a reasonably succinct and inspired manner. If they can't inspire you about their cause, what hope is there? The committee has a responsibility to look beyond smart presentations or perfect prepared budgets, and consider how they can support the cause, professionally and managerially. Just because a really needy case cannot do a three-year forecast doesn't mean that they aren't doing wonderful and important work. You could provide them with the financial expertise.

Time spent identifying the right partners and links is critical. I had a meeting with a major bank earlier this year who had decided to increase their commitment to education by £3 million per year. I emailed three very knowledgeable friends along the lines of: 'If you had £3 million every year to put into education where would you invest it?' They all responded within twenty-four hours with the most fascinating selection of small and medium front-line causes, none of which I had ever heard of and the bank staff certainly didn't know about.

Several of my friends and advisers are firmly in the 'only support small and medium-size charities' camp. It is important to spend quality time exploring opportunities, explaining the cause, enlisting the employees' involvement and answering their questions.

7. *Presentations*
Ask the shortlisted charities to present to the charity committee. Each charity should receive your brief: an outline of your company, including its work, number of employees, what it hopes to be able to bring to a partnership with a charity – the length of the partnership, the amount of money the employees feel they can raise, volunteering hours and management skills available and so on.

Each charity should be asked to present for no more than twenty-five minutes including: the background to the charity and the work it does; how the company's money will be used; what impact their support will have; opportunities for volunteering; management help they need; and how they can help the company raise money – perhaps by creating a new event or attracting a celebrity to a company fundraising event.

When the charity is chosen, both management teams should sit down and develop a plan for the duration of the partnership.

8. *Brainstorming ideas*
Now the fun part. You probably will not believe how much your company can do to help a cause or the community. And I suspect you will be amazed at how your staff and employees react to a proactive approach.

Now is the time to brainstorm opportunities and ideas with key people representing different business areas, including marketing, communications and human resources. Their mission is to think of opportunities in their area of work or business that will help raise money for the charity by establishing a link with current events and activities, and creating one or two new ones. Look for opportunities to fold in the charity to current company events, sponsorships, staff challenge activities, annual kick-off meetings. Wherever there is an opportunity to raise money or the profile of the charity and its beneficiaries. Consider creating a special and unique fundraising event.

If 100 employees can raise £500 each and the company matches their contribution, the total sum given to a charity – excluding Gift Aid – would be £100,000, costing the company £35,000. A real contribution to a charity and a very good investment by the company in its people and its reputation.

---

9. Other issues

Involving your clients in your good works will not only open up another avenue of dialogue, but also involve them in other opportunities to help the causes you have chosen. This can be particularly powerful at local level. It is also very effective in cementing and developing client relationships.

Most companies with a public face – retailers, airlines – are years ahead of others when it comes to **engaging customers**. They understand clearly that their relationship with their customers depends on a number of key facts, of which being actively involved in supporting good causes is an important part.

Consider **covering the programme's management costs** from company funds, so that all staff fundraising income and efforts goes directly to the cause. Please remember that charities do have overheads, that properly managed campaigns or events need people and that people have to be paid.

Decide on a **matching policy**. This is where the company decides to match the funds raised by their employees to an agreed limit. You also need to decide if this policy applies to people who raise money for a charity not included in the company's policy. And agree the **volunteering policy** (i.e. paid volunteer days).

Gifts in kind – such as used office furniture and computer equipment – are often appreciated.

Launching the new charity partnership throughout the company should be **high profile**. Information about the causes to be supported should be circulated with reasons, aims and targets. Senior management should visit key people and business areas and address company conferences to support the new initiative.

Celebrate success with great stories of daring and daft fundraising activities, and updates about the charity being funded.

10. *Measuring progress*
The company wants to make an impact on an issue or a charity. You should agree with the charity chosen at the start of the programme the impact you want to make. At the end of the year you must outline to your shareholders, employees and other stakeholders the progress made.

CASE HISTORY

HSBC Private Bank's partnership with Greenhouse Schools

Mark McCombe, the CEO of HSBC Private Bank, was keen for the bank to have a focused charitable policy, and particularly keen to engage the bank's staff in helping a specific charity.

The process
I interviewed the bank's directors individually to get their thoughts on adopting a single company charity, and other issues such as their preferred area of work, volunteering opportunities, fundraising and involving their clients. Encouragingly, they were all very supportive and enthusiastic, important because the charity committee and staff in the bank knew the programme had the full support of the CEO and directors.

A charity committee was formed consisting of twelve people from different operating parts of the business. Over the next few weeks they discussed which charitable area to focus on, eventually deciding to help disadvantaged young people between the ages of eleven and sixteen. They felt that this was the age group where young people faced the most challenges, were at their most vulnerable, and where outside support could potentially make a real difference to their future. They also wanted to support a small or medium-size charity where their involvement would make an impact.

Other issues to be decided included: how long the charity partnership should last (a two-year period was agreed); how much money the staff could raise through fundraising and how (a target of £200,000 was set, including matching from the bank); the volunteering opportunities available and how much time would the staff be allowed to take off for such work (two days paid each year). They also decided that they could lend managerial expertise in areas such as IT, accounts, financial education for young people, HR support, and work experience.

The charity committee prepared a briefing document for the charities chosen to pitch, including an outline of the bank's work, the number of employees and what they hoped to achieve from a partnership with a charity.

Researching the charities
Children and young people is one of the largest areas of charitable support. Using a number of contacts built up in the charity world, including senior members of grant-making trusts, active philanthropists and experts on disadvantaged children, thirty possible charities were selected. This

was then cut to ten – five medium, five small – and profiles were put forward to the charity committee.

The decision
The five shortlisted charities presented a general description of their work to the charity committee, how HSBC Private Bank could support them, fundraising ideas, and requests for volunteering and management support.

The bank finally decided on the Greenhouse Schools Project, a young charity that helps young people become involved in sport, dance and drama.

It was a great result and reward for three months of hard work. The charity committee felt that Greenhouse was just the job to inspire not only engagement by HSBC Private Bank's staff but also, in time, some of their clients.

Launching the partnership
Selling the charity partnership to all the employees was hugely important. The partnership was announced on the intranet by Mark McCombe. Greenhouse was invited to present to the main board and senior heads of department, which was a great success. There were also two launch parties at the bank's HQ.

The result?
Nine months after the charity partnership was launched it is working brilliantly.

Various members of the bank's staff have cycled from London to Bristol, and from London to Paris; twelve intrepid rowers re enacted the *Three Men in a Boat* trip by rowing the Thames between Kingston and Oxford; others have run the London Marathon, skydived and completed the gruelling 'Three Peaks Challenge'; raising an astonishing total of £150,000 (so far) for Greenhouse. And the bank's staff members have helped the charity with new branding, creating new marketing materials and redesigning their website.

Sarah Greer, head of the charity committee, says: 'Our partnership with the Greenhouse Schools project has been inspirational and motivational for our staff and for people at Greenhouse, too. Raising £150,000 in nine months is incredible and surpasses all our expectations from the start when we began the process of choosing a charity and developed a partnership plan. We've also enjoyed working closely with staff and children at Greenhouse to try and help the charity and the young people in as many different ways as we can.'

For Mike de Giorgio, the founder of Greenhouse: 'It has been a wonderful opportunity for a young charity to work with a significant company. It has allowed us to build a relationship with HSBC Private Bank that has helped us to develop the charity, not only by raising funds but also by engaging with their staff.'

CHANGE THE WORLD 9 TO 5

Published by the same team who created the We Are What We Do movement and gave us *Change the World for a Fiver*, this book gives suggestions and ideas for changing the world while you are at work, which, as they quite reasonably point out, is where we spend most of our waking lives. Apparently 65 per cent of UK business leaders said they would change their policies if pressed by their employees, so make your workplace more environmentally friendly – now!

Top 10 ideas based on actions taken and posted on www.wearewhatwedo.org.

1. **Say thanks.**
2. **Recycle waste paper.**
3. **Take the stairs.**
4. **Shut down your computer properly.**
5. **Enjoy a Fairtrade brew.**
6. **Practise good manners.**
7. **Praise people.**
8. **Turn away from your screen and ... blink.**
9. **Pull the plug on mobile phone chargers.**
10. **Remember people's names.**

Corporate Success Stories

I have chosen five examples of enlightened and extremely effective company charity programmes.

Two – Innocent Drinks and Richer Sounds – are highly successful and profitable entrepreneurial businesses. Both commit 10 per cent of their annual profits to their foundations, and their profits haven't suffered.

Reed Elsevier is an excellent example of an international company which is serious about its corporate responsibility and charity work.

ICAP's case proves what a City firm can do when led in an inspired manner.

And Marks & Spencer are doing now what most companies will be doing within five years, and have stolen a strong commercial and marketing advantage by acting ahead of their competitors.

As Richard Reed of Innocent says: 'In an era of growing consumer and employee awareness of the unintended consequences of capitalism, it is those companies who are the most responsible that will also be the most successful.'

Innocent Drinks

Richard Reed and his partners, Alan Balon and Jon Wright, met at Cambridge and always wanted to start their own business. They had absolutely no experience in the drinks market. They started Innocent after a now legendary experiment at a jazz festival where the drinks were sold and people asked to place their empty cups in a 'yes' or 'no' bin to vote whether the three should give up their jobs and make smoothies full-time. With the 'yes' bin recording a landslide victory they quit their jobs the next day. They raised £250,000 from venture capital and have never had to go back for more money. They own 70 per cent of the company, an original investor 'business angel' owns 20 per cent and the team who work for Innocent own 10 per cent between them.

Reed feels that one of the most important things in his company is pride: in producing a pure and special product; and in working for a company that treats its suppliers as partners. The organisation is great fun – its office is called Fruit Towers, their delivery vans are covered in grass, or camouflaged as cows, and their website is original and funny.

Behind the fun is a very carefully thought-through business. For the last three years the company's turnover has doubled each year to £100 million in 2006–7. They have received many takeover approaches but feel no desire to sell out, despite or perhaps because of the fact that they have 68 per cent market share, and their competitors are all 'big brands'.

The company makes only 100 per cent natural healthy products, 'putting fruit first' from environmentally and socially responsible sourced ingredients. The business uses green, clean power where necessary, and shares the wealth the company creates with the people who have helped create it and deserve it. Hence everyone at Innocent gets access to equity and a share in the profits, with an additional 10 per cent of profits going to their foundation.

From their first day in business, when they delivered fruit smoothies to the local homeless, Reed and his colleagues have built giving into the DNA of the company. The foundation's remit is to invest in the countries and communities where the fruit comes from; currently this involves working with projects as diverse as building keyhole gardens in Africa so communities have access to fresh fruit and veg, to educating kids in Costa Rica about the benefits of protecting their rainforests. Each year the company gives 10 per cent of profits to fund these projects and 2007 will see investment in eighteen projects round the world. As Reed says: 'With business, as in life, the more you give, the more you get.'

Innocent also supports Age Concern by arranging to fit mini-bobble hats on their smoothies, selling them at Sainsburys stores, and donating 50p on each sale to help keep people warm in the winter. This year their target is 400,000 little hats. Then there is their touring of village fêtes throughout the UK, making people smile through the power of Splat the Rat and coconut shies, culminating in the UK's biggest ever fête in Regent's Park in London. No wonder people like working there.

For a flavour and a smile visit: www.innocent drinks.co.uk.

ICAP

Michael Spencer, Group CEO and one of the founders of ICAP, started the company's Charity Day, and says: 'It is one of things that I am proudest about that we've achieved within this company. To me it is incredible to think that one day each year, in every one of our thirty-one centres around the globe, the staff that work for us don't work for themselves. They don't even work for the shareholders. They work for charities, and every year we raise millions of pounds for worthy causes and that makes me feel fantastic.'

ICAP'S Charity Day is a unique and inspired example of how a company can do enormous good for others if they put enough effort into it.

ICAP is the world's largest interdealer broker for commercial and investment banks, with an average daily transaction volume in excess of $1.5 trillion, 50 per cent of which is electronic.

ICAP had always given money to charity, but on an ad hoc basis. Then, in 1993, when the London office had grown to around 100 people, it decided to do something larger and more innovative. The idea of the ICAP Charity Day was born, a day on which all company revenues and brokers' personal commissions would be given away to just a few charities, meaning that each charity would receive a large amount of money that would make a real difference to their operations.

All of ICAP's offices around the world take part, and many of the staff wear fancy dress. The charities encourage as many of their celebrity patrons to attend the ICAP offices on the day to encourage the brokers and their customers. In the past, Prince William and celebrities such as England and Chelsea football players John Terry and Frank Lampard, as well as Sir Elton John and Sir Richard Attenborough have attended the London office. The New York office was lucky enough to have Denzel Washington, and Martina Navratilova, and some of the staff from the South African office were invited to attend a private reception with Nelson Mandela in order to present him with the cheque for the Nelson Mandela Aids Foundation. The Australian office entertained cricketer Steven Waugh for the day.

The charities chosen each year are put forward by staff and customers for selection. A committee then sits and agrees the final list, which tries to represent a variety of causes ranging from charities working for children and young people, to medical research and hospitals, cancer, education for the underprivileged or physically or mentally impaired, the Third World and conservation.

In 1993, ICAP raised £288,000. Over the years the amount raised grew until in 2006 they raised an astonishing £7.1 million in one day. A total of £33 million has been raised for charity by the company.

→ www.icap.com

Richer Sounds

CORPORATE GIVING

Julian Richer is a successful entrepreneur who has built up a chain of hi-fi shops, Richer Sounds. On the way he has become one of the wealthiest men in Britain, and his company has won numerous awards: for the most sales per square foot, for best customer service, and for being one of the best workplaces in the country.

He refers to his employees as colleagues. They all have direct access to him; there is an active suggestion scheme which rewards colleagues for their ideas; he has fourteen different properties throughout the UK and Europe, which he lets his colleagues use for free holidays; if employees are ill they can consult his doctor in Harley Street; and so on. It's a fun place to work, and is highly productive and profitable.

On top of all this, 10 per cent of the annual pre-tax profits of Richer Sounds go to The Persula Foundation, a registered charitable trust, which Julian established in 1994. Its main aims are:

- Actively to support existing charities and good causes in ways that add value to their work.
- To develop unique and innovative projects where a need is identified.
- To take fair and thoughtful decisions on funding applications with as little delay and bureaucracy as possible.
- Every application to the foundation is respected and answered.

Julian gives all his colleagues the opportunity to take time out from their work to support The Persula Foundation or any of the charities they may be currently supporting throughout the UK. The Persula Foundation currently has eight Generic Research Projects (GRPs) in human rights and welfare, animal welfare, blind and visually impaired, deaf and hard of hearing, mental health and learning disabilities, bullying, physical disabilities and youth issues.

The foundation supports many projects, including those that find fundraising more difficult, including the World Society for the Protection of Animals (WSPA) Humane Slaughter Project. WSPA are working towards establishing model humane slaughter training techniques in target regions, and work with governments, industry and academics to achieve measurable improvements in commercial slaughterhouses. The Persula Foundation's support will help bring an end to the cruellest animal farming practices.

The foundation also backs The Helen Bamber Foundation with a grant for a dedicated Women's programme providing practical help, care and treatment for women who have suffered human rights violations and been traumatised by their experiences and face barriers accessing appropriate forms of support.

Another Persula-supported charity is the MicroLoan Foundation (MLF), a UK-based organisation that provides small loans, basic business training and on-going mentoring support to poor people in sub-Saharan Africa to enable them to develop self-sustainable livelihoods, to feed, clothe and educate their families, and work their own way out of the poverty trap. The mission of MLF is significantly to reduce the depth and breadth of poverty in the communities within which it operates. Through Persula's support, MLF has provided funding for business loans in Malawi.

It is very advanced behaviour. But here comes the interesting bit. Julian believes that the major benefit the company receives from this considered approach to giving is in his colleagues' job satisfaction. The result is a company which is focused on the highest levels of customer service, making money, looking after its employees and being useful.

→ www.persula.org and www.richersounds.co.uk

M&S

Let's put our British cynicism to one side, because M&S has changed 'Corporate Responsibility' (which they were doing pretty well) into 'How We Do Business', and we all surmise they wouldn't be doing this at all if it didn't help their profits.

You have it in one. Acting responsibly and helping people beyond your own customer base is good business, and M&S is providing a brilliant example of just how good it can get.

Before the promotion of 'Look Behind the Label' in 2006 (sustainable fish/reduced packaging/reduced salt and more) M&S were already one of the leaders when it came to donating pre-tax profits to charity. Their latest report shows they give 1.9 per cent of pre-tax profits away, up from 1.51 per cent the previous year – which already placed them at number 11 in the UK's Giving List. And around 5 per cent of their staff give through their payroll against the UK norm of under 2 per cent.

But with Plan A, which was launched in early 2007, M&S have gone public in a huge way. It's a plan that touches every part of the business, their suppliers, their staff and every stakeholder. The Corporate Responsibility committee, which used to meet twice a year, has been replaced by the 'How We Do Business' committee, headed by CEO Stuart Rose, which meets monthly.

Do something well and shout about it. M&S has received accolades from organisations as diverse as the RSPCA for 'good business' and Greenpeace for sustainable fish supply, has been polled by the public as top retailer for food and fashion, and leading corporate responsibility company, moving skywards in various league tables for best workplace, responsible retailer and more. All of which is great publicity, a great staff motivator and, yes, good for business. More and more of us would rather shop somewhere where we can choose Fairtrade goods, home-grown produce, less packaging and fewer air-miles. (Research conducted by YouGov for M&S shows 73 per cent of their customers have changed their behaviour over a year in response to concerns about the environment.)

The depth and breadth of the campaign – with its 100 targets to make M&S the 'greenest retailer in the UK' by 2012 – is exemplary. If you doubt it, look up Anaerobic Digestion on their website (find it in Plan A/Waste – they correctly assumed I might not know what it meant!). A great self-explanatory cartoon on how waste is being recycled as fertiliser and biogas for renewable energy together with farm animal and slurry gushing sound effects!

During 2007 an average of three new Plan A initiatives have been press released every month. Influence is being extended by supporting the W.I.'s Carbon Challenge, (www.womens-institute.co.uk/carbonchallenge) hoping for at least 50,000 participants. It may be small beer set against over 15 million store visits a week, but reaching people in different ways through different initiatives makes for a great business. Performance targets have been set, progress reported and impact independently audited –

on the website for public consumption.

It helps that M&S is one of our leading companies and a visible, high street retailer. But let's pause and go back to the start. Stuart Rose watched *An Inconvenient Truth* (the Al Gore film on climate change) and within a few months held a private screening for his senior managers, whipped up their enthusiasm and put the plans in place. He could have sat back glowing in the success of the 'Look Behind the Label' and a charitable record to be proud about. Instead M&S has trail-blazed corporate responsibility to another level – a strategic business level – and for that we must all be grateful.

As Stuart Rose says: 'The science is compelling. We have to act now so that we live sustainably on our one and only planet. Doing nothing is not an option.'

→ www.marksandspencer.com

Reed Elsevier

Reed Elsevier is one of the largest publishers in the world of information for professional users. Each year it publishes more than 20,000 different magazines, books, CD-Roms and internet-based data and information services. Three things underpin the company's impressive corporate responsibility programme: leadership, values and the company's DNA.

Reed's corporate responsibility programme is led from the top. When Sir Crispin Davis became CEO of Reed Elsevier he recognised the social and business importance of running a large company that marched to a set of clear values, and set about introducing them. He says of that time: 'Morale was low. The business had gone through tough times. The business was assembled by acquisition so it was in silos. It screamed out for a set of core values and a consistent business philosophy that people could identify with and take pride in.'

A survey of employees throughout the group took place to find out what they thought should be the key values of the company. Five core values emerged: customer focus, a passion for winning, valuing people, innovation, no boundaries.

Corporate responsibility is being built into the DNA of the group, in every area of its work. There are five areas – governance, workplace, marketplace, community and environment – with aims for each, and at the end of the year the company reports on the impact made. It is both common sense and business sense, and it matters to Reed Elsevier, not least because the CEO says so. As Sir Crispin states: 'We are committed to making consistent improvements in how we conduct our business and manage our impact on stakeholders, from employees and customers to shareholders and governments, in communities and environments where we live and work ...

'The most significant impact to our business is in employee satisfaction. The matching gifts by the Elsevier Foundation and RE Corporate send a strong message to our employees that RE is a great place to work because it is willing to support the same charitable organisations which employees enthusiastically support. This leads to greater employee retention and also to increased productivity in the day-to-day work environment. Another business benefit is that locally sponsored events help RE gain greater visibility in its local communities through media coverage. This has a subtle impact on our ability to recruit new employees.'

Some Reed initiatives

It is interesting how some of the small initiatives supported by Reed's staff with both time and cash have grown from small 'seedlings' into rather substantial charities in their own right. And also how many useful projects take place each year throughout the world with a combination of staff enthusiasm and with relatively small sums of money.

Alexandra Scott, the daughter of an American Elsevier employee, passed away in August 2004, at the age of eight, after years of battling neuroblastoma, an aggressive childhood cancer. Alex started her first Lemonade Stand in July 2000 at the age of four to raise money for Paediatric Cancer Research. As a tribute to Alex, Reed Elsevier offices through the world are encouraged to hold their own lemonade stand on or around the anniversary of Alex's first stand. Reed businesses have contributed $111,000 over the last three years and a considerable amount of staff time. As impressively, **Alex's Lemonade Stand** has grown into a foundation which has so far raised over $12 million for childhood cancer research, and given millions of dollars for research across America (www.alexslemonade.com).

Staff from Reed Exhibitions flagship World Travel Exhibition created **Just a Drop** in 1998, an international charity to raise money to provide clean water and health education programmes. Since its inception the charity has assisted over 800,000 children in twenty-four countries and helped save the lives of thousands more. Four million children die every year from water-related diseases such as diarrhoea, dysentery and cholera; 1.4 billion children have no access to clean water close to their homes, yet a little over £1 buys a child clean water for ten years. A little money – Just a Drop – can make a big difference. To date the campaign has raised over £750,000 (www.JustADrop.org).

For the last seven years the company has worked with **Book Aid International**, and donated over one million books to schools and libraries to promote reading in the developing world, particularly Sub-Saharan Africa. They also contribute towards developing libraries and their staff worldwide also donate thousands of their own books during a 'bring a book week'.

Numerous other small and practical projects initiated by Reed staff throughout the world include: cleaning up a shelter for underprivileged children and providing new furniture in Malaysia; giving financial support for a school for children who are mostly orphans and who have special needs in Uganda; and working with a charity to improve education and the environment in the slums of Rio de Janeiro.

In the UK employees at HQ supported a local day centre for the homeless, **Connections at St Martin's**, providing cash towards the redevelopment of their site, and helping out in myriad other ways – organising football matches and supplying the strip, supporting an art project (the finished painting went up in HQ), and a sailing programme.

Another group of over 100 staff revamped the **Children's Trust** garden area to provide children with multiple disabilities with an outdoor space where they could enjoy the objects, sights and sounds around them. Teams renovated each of the themed areas including the Tadworth farm, sound garden, magic circus, Wizard of Oz garden, teepee trail, sensory garden and outer space, persuading local companies to donate most of the tools and materials used. Family and friends also raised £5,350 towards the rebuilding of the brain injury unit at the trust. At the end of the day the marketing director who organised the event was moved enough to remark that 'she had a tear in her eye when one of the children went round the nature trail in his wheelchair – and very proud to be part of such a great enthusiastic team.'

The final word rests with Sir Crispin: 'Community represents an integral part of how we do business. Contributing to our global communities is both an opportunity and a responsibility. It helps us inspire employees, positively aid beneficiaries, improve our reputation and meet our obligations as one of the world's largest publishers. Consequently, our global community programme, Reed Elsevier Cares, has as its mission, "to play a positive role in our local and global communities, primarily through employee involvement". We focus on education for disadvantaged young people and community initiatives of importance to local employees.'

→ www.reed-elsevier.com

Epilogue

A FORCE OF NATURE

'This is the true joy in life . . . Being used by a purpose recognised by yourself as a mighty one . . . Being a force of nature instead of a feverish, selfish little clod of ailments and grievances complaining that the world will not devote itself to making you happy. I am of the opinion that my life belongs to the whole community and as long as I live it is my privilege to do for it whatever I can. I want to be thoroughly used up when I die. For the harder I work the more I live. I rejoice in life for its own sake. Life is no brief candle for me. It is a sort of splendid torch which I've got to hold up for the moment, and I want to make it burn as brightly as possible before handing it on to future generations.'

George Bernard Shaw

It's a great line, isn't it? 'Being a force of nature instead of a feverish, selfish little clod of ailments and grievances complaining that the world will not devote itself to making you happy.'

So what will you actually DO now? Whose lives will you change? Will you give more? Start to focus your charitable involvement in a more effective way? Look for quiet ways to help friends? Of course, my hope is that you will have been inspired, and intrigued enough to do more to help others, and by doing so discover a generosity of spirit within yourself that makes you glow, and feel there is a

EPILOGUE

point to you. For the truth is that just a little money and a small dollop of kindness can go a long way and enrich your own life immeasurably. It's interesting that 'happiness gurus' have not thought of measuring the relationship between happiness and giving. They should.

I wrote this book because I have personally experienced the positive benefits of giving. It made a huge impact on me and on others who gave, as well as the lives of those who received, of course. I have witnessed many acts of real love, humility and generosity, as well as moments of gratitude, all of which made me feel good, touched me deeply and made me feel better about the world. I have watched how giving has bought out the very best in people, itself inspiring. That literally the more you give to life, the more you get back.

I want to encourage you to do the same, especially those who are 'thinking' of doing something useful, whether you are an individual or run a company.

I would love your feedback. Maybe you could tell me about some of the things that you have done to help or to serve people, or a remarkable achievement by someone you know. Write to me or send an email – both to encourage me, and so that I can pass on some of your stories to inspire others. If I get enough great tales I might even publish a book of them (with your permission, of course!).

The More You Give, The More You Get isn't just a book. We encourage and advise individuals, and companies, about how to give imaginatively and effectively. We search out great causes, doing wonderful work who need more funding to continue their work, and who we know will use the money effectively and well.

We work with an informal network of knowledgeable people, trusts and organisations who give, have good hearts,

237

EPILOGUE

like 'getting things done' and want to make a difference.

The most rewarding work is matching individuals and companies with exciting, worthwhile and often innovative projects that might otherwise remain undiscovered because they lack the resources to search for funds in the way that well-known charities can do. These are projects where the donors can make a significant and long-term impact, and it is an enormously exciting time, when the donors become both moved and enthused, a moment when great things are possible. We can then 'light the touch paper and retire'.

If you, or your company, would like to discuss any aspect of effective charitable giving, or to create an inspiring charity programme, contact us on enquiries@themoreyougive.co.uk.

The More You Give
59A Portobello Road
London W11 3DB
→ www.themoreyougive.co.uk

" To laugh often and much; to win the respect of intelligent people, and the affection of children; to earn the appreciation of honest critics and endure the betrayal of false friends; to appreciate beauty, to find the best in others; to leave the world a bit better, whether by a healthy child, a garden patch or a redeemed social condition; to know that even one life has breathed easier because you have lived. This is to have succeeded. "   Ralph Waldo Emerson